KU-067-111

Tynwyd o S...
Withdrawn from stock

THE BIG BOOK
OF BREWING

The Big Book of Brewing

by

DAVE LINE

GWASANAETH LLYFRGELL CLWYD

RHIF
DOSBARTH
CLASS NUMBER

RHIF COPI. COPY No.
P 2708
RHIF LLYFRWERTHWR
BOOKSELLER No.
ME

CLWYD LIBRARY SERVICE

Cover picture: GINA HARRIS
Illustrations: DAVE LINE AND REX ROYLE
Photographs: B. BEESLEY

© "The Amateur Winemaker" Publications Ltd.
Andover, Hants.

SBN 0 900841 34 6

First Impression	-	-	-	January 1974
Second Impression		-	-	June 1976
Third Impression	-	-	-	January 1978
Fourth Impression		-	-	January 1979
Fifth Impression	-	-	-	November 1979
Sixth Impression	-	-	-	August 1980
Seventh Impression		-	-	July 1981
Eighth Impression		-	-	April 1982
Ninth Impression	-	-	-	November 1982

Printed in Great Britain by :
Standard Press (Andover) Ltd., South Street, Andover, Hants.
Telephone : 52413

Contents

ADVANCED RECIPES

Introduction

HOME BREWING has established itself over the last decade as one of the most popular national pastimes. The success of the hobby was not hard to foresee and was indeed really only born out of necessity. You can steal a man's wife, burn down his house, sack him from his job, but never should you deny him the right to sup good ale! It is a tribute to our heritage that we are always prepared to seek out a source of good beer.

Gone are the days when you got a decent pint of acceptable strength at your "local". The present laws of the country penalise strong beer with heavy taxation, and with shareholders to please, the accountants in the big breweries seem to have more influence on the quality of the beer than the brewers themselves. Quality has fallen as specifications become so tight and unyielding from these economic pressures. Nowadays, beer is such a unified product that it is virtually impossible to distinguish between brand names. Regrettably, as well, nobody in the commercial field seems bothered over the customer's reaction to these weak expensive drinks.

This is where home brewing comes into the picture. As good beer is rapidly becoming "extinct" commercially, the only way to ensure a good supply is to brew it yourself. Considering that it is possible to make a gallon of top quality ale for less than the price of a pint at your "local" it is hardly surprising that thousands of dissatisfied beer lovers join the craft each year. Their enthusiasm has sparked off a multi-million industry to satisfy the needs in respect of ingredients, equipment and information.

11

Many excellent books have been written on the subject of home brewing which have been instrumental in raising the standard and quality up to, and in some cases, higher than commercial beers.

One criticism often levelled at home brewed beer is that the taste is "different" from accepted commercial varieties. Remarks are made on the characteristic malty tang that predominates in the flavour of most home brewed beer, with the result that one needs to acquire the palate for these drinks.

Most of these criticisms can be traced back to the malt extract syrups that are used in the majority of these beers. Most concentrated malt syrups, whether used in conjunction with other ingredients, or as an integral part of a beer kit, impose severe limitations on flavour and quality. During manufacture, the concentration process destroys many of the desirable features necessary for a good beer wort. Obviously one cannot expect a top quality lager and stout to be brewed from the same malt syrup. Good draught beer is also difficult to brew using these techniques.

In all fairness, malt extract and beer kits do provide a means of brewing a cheap drinkable beer without expending too much time and effort.

In fact, the progression through from beer kits and malt extract brews to "grain" beers is just the natural path of evolution of home brewing. By starting with these basic methods, many brewers have served a useful apprenticeship by learning and understanding the techniques of brewing. Over this period a successful method of making beers by the professional way, as practised by the commercial breweries, has been the elusive goal of these home brewers.

This "Big Book of Brewing" is a breakthrough in technique, and suggests for the first time in the short history of modern home brewing a simple successful method of mashing barley malt so that the finest quality beers can be brewed as a matter of course.

All that is needed to achieve these successes is to take home brewing one stage further to produce your own "malt extract". The extra time spent in carrying out this "mashing" stage is probably less than you take over supping a couple of pints of your home-brew.

Have you ever tried mashing or making a "grain" beer?

If the answer is yes, then you can probably recollect an occasion that ended up with no beer, an irate wife, a backache, a bad temper, and a mass of sticky, useless grains!

Unfortunately, experiences like these have been so common that many home brewers have tried mashing in their quest for quality beer, found it difficult, and returned to the inferior, but much easier made malt extract brews. The stories about mashing have been perfectly true and have left grain beers with a bad reputation. Quite justifiably, I might add, as even I can vouch that mashing used to be such a messy and time consuming exercise that it was not really worth the effort.

Disillusioned home brewers attributed these failures to the difficulty in controlling the temperature during mashing to within a few degrees of 150°F. Experience has proved that these problems were more likely to be due to incorrect acidity, and inefficient mashing equipment rather than the temperature.

Mashing is now easy

Really the early failures in mashing techniques were due to our inexperience. Taking the easy way out we tried too hard to copy and scale down the commercial process without first sorting out the theory.

As it happens, temperature control is not so critical, and indeed 10°F out can be tolerated so long as you observe some simple rules. Custom built home brew equipment is now available to automatically look after the brew with the assurance of complete success. To get set up does not take long either.

Thus a few minutes extra work can at last bring within your grasp beers of the highest quality and possessing the finest flavour.

By following the practices recommended in this book, you can produce a beer far superior to that made using other home brewing methods. Indeed, it would not be an exageration to say that the best commercial breweries would be pushed to match the quality of your ales.

The only people likely to brew a beer as good as yourself are fellow home brewers who will of course, be using the same techniques!

The difference in the finished beer is quite remarkable. Tastes and flavours almost forgotton become reality again.

Mashing leaves you "free to do whatever you like . . ."

Pale Ales, Lights, Lagers, Browns and Milds can be brewed exactly as you wish to suit your own palate and not how some accountant deems you should like. Draught Bitters and Stouts, and even beer "from the wood" can be brewed with ease to give the ultimate satisfaction and rewards from home brewing.

RECIPES IN THIS BOOK

BROWN ALES

SWEET STOUTS

MEDICINAL STOUT

DRY STOUTS

BARLEY WINES

SHANDY

THE LANGUAGE OF THE BREWER!

THE brewing industry is steeped in tradition and has protected the centuries old terminology devised and used by the past masters of the art.

Not knowing the origins, or understanding some of these words only adds to the confusion for beginners to home brewing, so I have tried to use more familiar terms. Through experience, though, some of the brewing terms have been found to be the most descriptive and appropriate for the particular case, and hence these terms, which have been defined below, have been used extensively in the book.

ATTENUATION

The thinning of the beer during fermentation through the conversion of the heavy malt sugars in solution to the lighter alcohol: the decrease in specific gravity as noted by a hydrometer.

ADJUNCTS
Grain starches, such as maize, rice, or wheat that are added to the grist to supplement the fermentable extract.

BARREL
36 gallons, or a cask containing 36 gallons. Or, if you are Irish, 32 gallons!

CONDITION
Referring to hops, it is the yellow, sticky powder on the petals that provides a visual guide for assessing the quality of the hop.

CONDITION
In the bottle, condition is the release of dissolved carbon dioxide gas which gives the beer the "fizz" and sparkle.

CONDITIONING
The process of producing the carbon dioxide gas in the beer.

CUTTING
Arresting the fermentation by adding finings.

FINING
To clear the beer artificially.

FININGS
Gelatine or Isinglass.

GOODS
The mixture of crushed grain, adjuncts and water in the mash tun.

GRIST
The dry mixture of crushed grain and adjuncts prior to mashing.

GRAVITY
Specific gravity: the ratio of weight of a solution to an equal volume of water. A measure of the amount of sugar and means of assessing the alcohol potential of the beer

HYDROMETER
Instrument for measuring specific gravity.

INITIAL HEAT

The temperature of the goods immediaafter tely mixing the malt and hot water.

KICKING

A vigorous boiling action.

KRAUSEN WORT

Small quantity of fermenting wort added to a bulk of beer, prior to bottling or casking, to create natural conditioning.

LENGTH

Literally means "volume".

LIQUOR

Not the "hard stuff", just mere drinking water

PITCHING

Adding the yeast to the wort.

PRIMING

Adding sugar or wort to beer to promote secondary fermentation for conditioning in the bottle or cask.

RIGHT ARM

Used for drinking your brew.

RUNNINGS

The worts drawn off the mash-tun.

SKIMMING

Removing the surplus yeast and undesirable substances from the surface of the beer.

SPARGE

To spray, or rinse the sweet wort from the mashed grain with hot water.

STRIKE HEAT

The temperature of the water prior to mixing it with the grain for mashing.

TURBID

Cloudy.

WORT

The sweet malt solution sparged from the mashed grain.

CHAPTER 1

The commercial
brewing process

BREWING is a highly developed craft which has reached its perfection from centuries of practice and research. This chapter is a brief outline of the commercial process of brewing beer, from the choice of ingredients to the finished product. From this we can extract the relevant points to suit our plastic dustbin breweries.

It is not meant as a chance for you to gain the necessary "know-how" to enable you to rush the plans off to your local Planning Authority to convert your three-bedroomed semi into a Two-Quarter Brewery turning out a thousand barrels of beer a year! No matter how admirable the sentiment may be, you won't get away with it.

Beer is basically brewed from barley, hops, yeast and water, which are all honest-to-goodness products of nature. Barley and hops are particularly sensitive to changes in climatic and soil conditions, and therefore, openly defy most of the strict quality control methods that can be imposed by this modern world. The production of these ingredients has developed into highly specialised, skilful, but separate industries from the actual brewing process.

The big commercial breweries mostly leave these preliminary tasks to the farmers and hop growers, since they are only really interested in the finished ingredients. Raw Barley has no brewing value until it has been malted and although most breweries have traditionally produced their own malt the modern trend is also to leave this task to the experts.

Malting is the process of germination and drying which converts the inside of the raw barley grain to a form of starch that can be converted into soluble malt sugars in the brewhouse.

Like the professionals, we are only really interested in these ingredients when all the hard work has been done! I suppose you could plough up your vegetable patch in favour of a spread of barley and have hop bines trained around the front door porch, but I doubt if the returns and response of others would make the venture worthwhile.

The barley malt and the hops are kept in cool, dry, dark store rooms in the brewery until they are ready for use. Before brewing, the malt is weighed, crushed and mixed with small proportions of other grains, such as maize, rice and wheat to form the grist.

The grist is mixed with hot water and fed via a chute into a large pre-heated copper vessel known as a mash-tun. The temperature of the water is carefully calculated so that the hot infusion with the grain settles out to about 150°F. In these conditions, enzymes in the malt are activated which convert the starch to fermentable sugar. The temperature of the mixture, known as the "goods", and the length of time of mashing, can be altered to suit the type of beer being brewed.

The mash-tun has a perforated false bottom through which the sweet wort can be filtered from the grain husks after the completion of mashing. To ensure that all the malt sugars are extracted, the grains are sprayed (sorry, "sparged" in brewery language!) with hot water from arms perforated with small holes that rotate above the surface of the mash.

The sweet wort is then pumped to large coppers where it is boiled, together with sugar and hops, for about one and a half hours. It is the boiling action that brings about the marriage of flavours between the sweet malt and the bitter hops that is such a desirable characteristic of beer.

After straining and cooling, the wort is pumped to the fermentation vessel. Various systems of fermentation are used, but the most common type for English top fermenting ales is the Skimming system. The beer is fermented in a plain open topped tank, and it is this method that is easiest for home-brewers to copy with their plastic dustbins.

Before the yeast is added, the gravity or alcohol potential is measured by the brewer using a hydrometer. The reading is checked by a Customs Official, who subsequently uses the figure to assess the Excise Duty payment. The duty averages about 5p per pint of beer. Home-brewers are exempt from this taxation since they are not entitled to sell their produce. In fact it is highly illegal to sell beer without a licence, and the penalties for doing so can be very severe.

The wort is then pitched with yeast, a low form of plant life, which has the ability to change the malt sugar into alcohol and carbon dioxide gas. The yeast, feeding on the sugars, multiplies and forms a thick frothy meringue-like head on the fermenting wort. The covering provides a barrier to any airborne infection. Excess yeast formed by the reproduction process is skimmed off, along with any extraneous matter.

The action of fermentation generates heat in the fermentation vessel. Cooling is effected by cold water radiator pipes called attemperators inside the vessel.

After two or three days, when the yeast has used up about three quarters of the available sugar, the "green" beer is rough filtered off into storage tanks. Finings are added and the beer is allowed to clear and mature. The maturation time and all subsequent treatment help to determine the type of beer produced.

Bottled and keg beer do not benefit from a long maturation period and are filtered again, pasteurised, chilled and artificially carbonated as soon as possible, and with the exception of obvious differences in dispensing equipment, they can be regarded as the same. Naturally conditioned bottled beers, with the notable exception of one well-known stout, are almost an extinct breed in the commercial field. The high quality, fine flavoured, naturally conditioned beers will soon, unfortunately, only be produced by home-brewers.

Most draught beers are still naturally conditioned. The old fashioned wooden barrels, like naturally conditioned bottled beer, are economic thorns in the side of brewery accountants, and are similarly being phased out of use. Casks nowadays are made from metal with glass linings. The beer is dispensed by carbon dioxide gas pressure injectors which force the natural conditioned beer up to the bar pumps.

From the bar pumps, the price of a pint will be more than what it costs you to make a gallon of the same type beer. Your beer will be stronger and better flavoured, and brewed as you like it, and not as someone else thinks you should like it.

But let us not be complacent over our home-brewed beer. The commercial breweries perfected the methods for producing the finest quality beers, and all we are doing is benefiting from their long experience and using these methods they have been forced to drop through economic pressures. For the relatively small quantities we are contemplating brewing, many of the above processes can either be eliminated or drastically simplified so that the finest quality beers can easily be produced at home with the minimum of time, experience and equipment, but with the maximum pride and personal satisfaction.

CHAPTER 2

Equipment

MILLIONS of gallons of high quality beer have been made over the centuries by people who did not possess the modern labour saving aids of electricity, gas, plastic and glass. Even when thermometers and hydrometers became available, old time brewers initially shunned these instruments, and regarded them as an intrusion on their personal skill. Mashing has been reborn as a method of making beer at home, so I have endeavoured to give the fullest details on the type of equipment that will be needed.

BRUHEAT BOILER

Brewing embraces many separate processes carried out at just as many temperature points. Mashing, Sparging, Boiling and Fermentation all have one thing in common in that the vessels used for the processes should be of about the same capacity as the volume of beer to be brewed. Brewing boilers, plastic containers and fermenting bins are readily available from home brew stockists for these purposes. And indeed, on the market are brewing boilers which are capable of dealing with *all* these tasks.

One of these integral all purpose boilers is the Bruheat marketed by Ritchie Products of Rolleston Road, Burton-on-Trent, which is basically a 5 gallon plus capacity polypropy-bucket fitted with a kettle type heating element controlled by a very accurate thermostat.

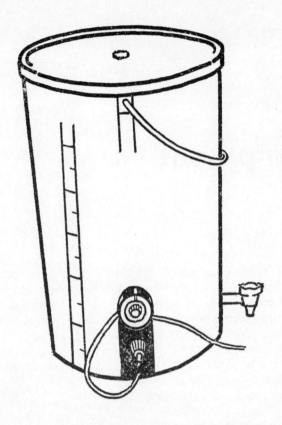

Although the bucket is 'plastic' it can withstand temperatures way in excess of boiling point and will not distort. The $2\frac{3}{4}$ kw. heating element has an automatic cut-out which isolates the electrical supply and cuts off the heating if the boiler boils dry, an important safety factor which I confirmed as satisfactory by a practical test.

The plate type thermostat has a dial setting 0 to 10 and covers a temperature range from about 50°F to boiling point. Since the dial is not calibrated in degrees of temperature it is a good idea to find the dial setting corresponding to the process temperatures used.

Simply fill the boiler with three gallons of water and suspend a thermometer in it. Switch on the heat with the dial set to 10 and raise the water temperature up to, for instance 150°F for mashing. Turn back the dial until the thermostat can be heard to click on and off. Record the dial setting (usually around 3½) for future reference.

In practice the temperature will cycle about 5°F above and below this figure when mashing because of the viscosity of the grain 'porridge'. So long as the temperature does not rise too much above the 150°F in the first few minutes no harm will be done.

Maximum heat is when the dial is set to 10 as for in the boiling process. The accurate thermostat has another side benefit. Even when selected for boiling the thermostat only permits pulses of electric current to the element, e.g. heat on for 10 seconds, off for 5 seconds. Thus although the element is in direct contact with the boiling wort the surafce temperature of the metal is prevented from rising too high and caramelising the wort and altering its flavour.

Being a free standing boiler with an integral heating element it can be used anywhere near an electric power point. Boiling the wort and hops outside the kitchen instead of in will prevent the house smelling like a brewery for a day after you brew up. Also being able to ferment the brew in a cold outhouse or garage has many advantages. All this praise about the boiler will make you think—where is the snag? Well, there is a slight one.

A normal mash using seven or eight pounds of grain can be a messy mixture if not handled sensibly. After the completion of the mashing process it is not practical to boil the grains with the hops. The sweet rich wort must be strained off to be used with hops. Unfortunately the tap gets blocked if you attempt to draw off the wort whilst it is still in the boiler. The obvious remedy is to contain the grain in some form of straining bag within the boiler but this does not work in practice. The bag can burn on the heated element and the mashing reactions can be nullified by the loss of heat circulation. Mashing must be done 'loose in the boiler'. Afterwards the grain must be transferred to another vessel for straining off and this is where a grain bag is useful. Using a bucket with a tap and the bag inside is a most satisfactory arrangement.

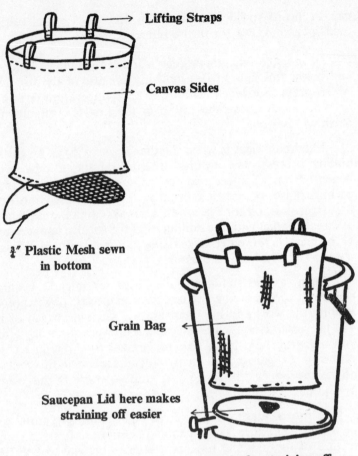

Lifting Straps

Canvas Sides

¾" **Plastic Mesh sewn
in bottom**

Grain Bag

**Saucepan Lid here makes
straining off easier**

**Ready for straining off.
The Grain Bag contained
in a bucket**

GRAIN BAG

The bag should have a capacity of around 4 gallons. For an efficient extraction of wort the side walls need to be made of some strong, fairly imperious material such as sail cloth or canvas. Plastic diamond mesh (⅛"/3 mm) as sold in gardening shops makes an ideal sieve for the bottom. Four loop straps attached to the side walls are used for carrying the bag or suspending it above the boiler if necassery for sparging.

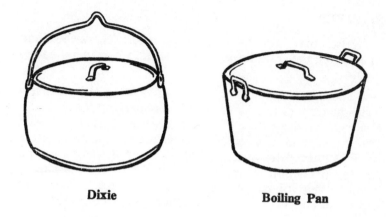

Dixie   Boiling Pan

DIXIE OR BOILING PAN

A large boiling pan as used by many home brewers already can be used for mashing. The method needs more supervision as will be explained later but it works perfectly adequately. Preferably the pan should have a capacity of at least 4 gallons if you are contemplating brewing 5 gallon batches of beer.

INSULATED CHEST

Certain large camping insulated chests can be used for the mashing process. Check first that the container can withstand water temperatures up to 180°F. The techniques are simplicity itself. Just add water around 175°F to the 'insulated mash tun' to preheat it and then pitch in the malt grain when the temperature falls to 165°F. After mixing, the temperature should stabilise around 150°F and the insulating properties of the chest will retain the heat for a couple of hours to ensure the mashing reactions are completed. Chests like the Amoco BL 548 with a tap at the bottom are best, but the more readily available Glovenzana Style 'Frigo' 16 and 22 litre chests without taps can be used although the goods need transferring to a grain bag for straining off after mashing.

27

SPARGER

After mashing, the malt sugars must be washed and rinsed from the grain husks by a procedure known as "sparging".

The sparger is just a means of holding the relatively large quantity of hot water needed for sparging coupled with a device for dispensing it in a fine spray. The water must also be kept at a reasonably constant temperature. More water is needed for sparging than is used in the mash-tun. An approximation is that the water needed for sparging is equal to the volume of the finished beer, e.g. making five gallons of beer will call for five gallons of sparge water.

Plastic pressure barrels, if you can find one empty of your home-brew, make ideal spargers. Another choice, the five gallon ex-wine polythene cube, kept in its cardboard container, is just as efficient and is easy to handle and provides better heat insulation than the barrel. So long as they are treated sensibly and are regularly inspected for damage, they will last for many a brew. You may prefer, however, to use a barrel which is constructed more rigidly of stronger plastic and in which any defect will be immediately visible.

The water should fall on the mashed grains as a fine spray for maximum effectiveness. After many tests, I settled for using the small rose from an indoor plant watering can attached to the tap of the sparge container with a two foot length of rubber tubing.

A simple and effective set-up for sparging, as described above

28

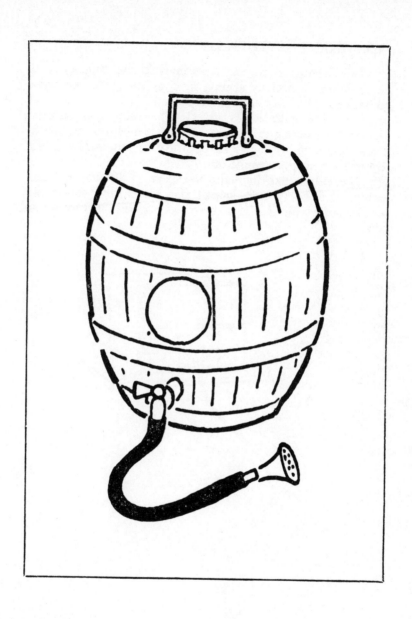

"EX WINE" POLYTHENE CUBE

Off-Licences and some supermarkets are supplied with cheap wines, especially sherry, in non-returnable polythene containers. They are square shaped and have a capacity of just over five gallons (25 litres). The semi-rigid cube is incased by a strong cardboard box for protection and mechanical handling with just an aperture for the screw fitting cap which incorporates the tap.

The cubes take up valuable space in the shops when empty, and being non-deposit containers, the shops are usually quite willing to give them away or sell them for a few pence

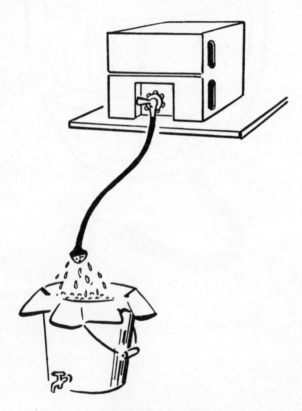

... used for sparging

Two or three of these containers are invaluable for home-brewing as secondary fermentation vessels, spargers and racking containers. They are remarkably robust and perfectly safe for the short storage times contemplated with our beers.

DUSTBIN

A plastic dustbin of at least 5 gallon capacity is essentia for a home-brewer. They are inexpensive, light, easy to clean and make ideal fermentation vessels. The black, heavy density ones are the safest and best.

There have been doubts cast on the suitability of some of the cheaper dustbins for home brewing regarding the stability of the chemical filler used in the manufacture for binding the plastic.

When the problem first came to light, I asked the advice of a chemist friend as to the suitability of my cheap dustbin. From his remarks, it seems that, seeing that I survived the first brew when the majority of toxic substances are leached out into the beer, I should live to brew many more gallons of ale!

Although many home-brewers have had the same experience, it pays to be on the safe side and buy the heavy duty bins. Special white home-brewing bins can now be purchased in some chain stores.

For easy measurement, the outside of the dustbin can be calibrated and marked in its capacity in gallons with intermediate marks for quarts.

OTHER EQUIPMENT

1 gallon jars—for storage of beer during the secondary fermentation.

Rubber bungs and airlocks for above
Pint or quart beer bottles
Plastic pressure barrel
Plastic funnels
Crown capper and caps
Siphon tube

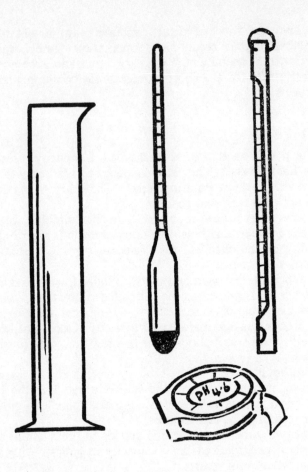

Thermometer in brass tube
Plastic spoons
Cleaning utensils
Kitchen scales, saucepans
Hydrometer and jar
Iodine
pH papers.

Most of the above equipment is self explanatory and details will be dealt with later in the appropriate sections in the book.

CHAPTER 3

Your first brew

AFTER grasping something of the basic knowledge of brewing, you are probably raring to have a go at making your first brew. If you are only interested in knowing "how" to make a decent pint of beer and not so much "why" we carry out the various procedures, then you should just follow the simple instructions laid down in this chapter.

You don't need to be a professional brewer, microbiologist, chemist or mathematician to brew good beer. In fact I regard it as a disadvantage to be a specialist in any of the vocations, since it is a natural tendency to concentrate too much attention on one particular aspect of brewing and neglect all other sections.

In my own case I found this to be true when I was experimenting to find a reliable method for keeping the temperature constant during mashing. My skills as an electrical engineer were applied to designing a fully transistorised control system which could maintain the temperature of the mash to a fraction of a degree of the required value.

In doing this, I completely overlooked that I could maintain the temperature in a much simpler way by using the water bath principle, or by mashing in an heat insulated container. Simple, I know, but *I* missed the obvious, and so did thousands of other home-brewers who also tried to perfect a technique for mashing. Once the idea had occurred to me, I set out to perfect it, and it is the central theme of this book.

THE SIMPLE BREWING METHOD

The best way to learn a new practice is actually to "do-it-yourself". In our case, the thought of ending up with five gallons of best bitter should be enough incentive to encourage you to do it right the first time.

The following procedure demonstrates the practical method involved in making a typical grain beer using the above equipment.

The hardest part is obviously in following the unfamiliar procedure for the first time and using ingredients and equipment that you have not handled before, but by carefully following the instructions, no problems should be experienced.

RECIPE FOR 5 GALLONS OF BITTER BEER

6 lb. Crushed Pale Malt
½lb. Cracked Crystal Malt
1lb. Demerara Sugar
3 ozs. Goldings Hops
Beer Yeast

MASHING USING BRUHEAT BOILER

1. Fill the boiler with 3 gallons of water. Add one teaspoonful of Gypsum and half a teaspoonful of Epsom Salts and stir until dissolved. Suspend a thermometer in the water.

2. Switch on the heat by selecting the dial setting to 10 and raise the temperature of the water to around 140°F. Stir in the crushed pale and crystal malts and ensure they are thoroughly dissolved to leave no dry spots.

3. With the heat still on, continuously stir in the grain mix until the temperature reaches 150°F and then wind back the dial setting until the thermostat clicks off.

4. Left on this setting the boiler will automatically look after the mashing process for the two hours or so that it takes to complete the starch conversion.

5. When mashing is over transfer the grain to the grain bag already positioned in a bucket. Alternatively, the grain bag can be arranged to be suspended by its straps over the boiler so the wort can fall directly into it. The technique is to transfer the mashed grain from the boiler to another bucket, or as I do, to a 5 gallon plastic fermenting bin. Two chairs are then placed seats towards the boiler on opposite sides. Using two broomsticks resting on the chair backs the grain bag is suspended by its straps just inside the boiler. The grain can now be put in the bag ready for sparging.

MASHING USING DIXIE

1. Fill the dixie with two and a half gallons of water. Add one teaspoonful of Gypsum and half a teaspoonful of Epsom Salts and stir in until dissolved. Suspend a thermometer in the water.

2. Apply heat and raise the temperature up to above 140°F and stir in the crushed grains until dissolved.

3. Stir continuously and with the heat still on raise the temperature of the grain mix up to 150°F.

4. Switch off the heat to allow the mash to react. Occasionally over the next one and a half hours return the cooled grains back to 150°F.

5. When the mashing is over transfer the grain for sparging as suggested in the Bruheat procedure.

SPARGING

1. Heat up five gallons of water to between 170 and 180°F and transfer it to the "Ex wine" polythene cube or pressure barrel sparger.

2. Ideally the sparger should be situated on a shelf or similar position to give about one foot head of pressure above the grain bag.

3. Having sensibly repositioned the equipment for sparging, collect the first turbid worts which drain off naturally or are collected after the bucket tap is opened and return them gently to the top of the grains. Repeat this procedure until the grains have formed a filter bed and the wort is running reasonably bright. About one quart of the cloudy wort needs to be returned before this is achieved.

4. Fit the sparge spray attachment to the sparger vessel and start sparging the grains, by opening the tap. Adjust the flow rate to give a gentle even spraying action. The sparge flow should also be adjusted to balance the outflow from the grain bag. Sparging must not be hurried.

5. The sparging operation will take 15 minutes or so to collect almost six gallons of wort. This time is not wasted since the worts can be run directly into the boiler and the temperature raised to boiling point ready for the addition of the hops and sugar.

BOILING

1. Boiling ideally calls for at least a five gallon boiler. If you only possess a smaller boiler then the wort must be boiled in stages. The hops can be added to the first fraction and the sugar to the second, though you may care to leave a few hops in the second as well. For clarity though, the rest of the procedure assumes that a large boiler is available.

2. When the wort is boiling vigorously, add the sugar and hops. The sugar must be added slowly, so that it can be dissolved by the boiling, rolling action of the wort, to prevent it from burning on the boiler bottom.

3. Prolong the boil until the volume of beer has been evaporated to five gallons. During boiling, which should last between one, and one and a half hours, the flavouring and preservative characteristics of the hops, are

married with that of the sweet wort. The wort must be boiled vigorously, and not just stewed, so that particles of cloudy protein matter can gum together and precipitate out to leave the liquid clear.

4. Switch off after boiling and allow the wort to cool for a few minutes so that the hops can sink to the bottom of the boiler and form a filter bed. Open the boiler tap and strain off the wort through the hop bed into a bucket. Finally, transfer the wort from the bucket to a plastic dustbin. Sprinkle the hops in the boiler with two kettlefuls of boiling water to release the absorbed extract.

5. Replace the lid of the dustbin loosely and allow the wort to cool as rapidly as possible.

FERMENTATION

1. When the wort has cooled to 55-60°F add the yeast, preferably made up as a starter (see Page 164). It should be shaken first, to return all the yeast sediment and head back into a milky solution. Be careful that the gas liberated by shaking does not build up and expend its wrath in giving you a yeast face-pack. The beer needs the yeast more than yourself!

2. Aerate the wort after pitching the yeast by stirring with a wooden spoon for a few minutes.

3. The fermentation should ideally be conducted in a place where the temperature remains cool (55-60°F) and reasonably constant all the time. Hot airing cupboards and green-houses are definitely not suitable places for fermenting beers.

4. The lid of the dustbin should be replaced to protect the yeast from airborne infection until the yeast has reproduced sufficiently to generate a protective crust over the surface.

5. The yeast crop will build up to a rocky head after about 24 hours. When the head flattens "pat" off the oxidised scum with the back of a wooden spoon and scrape off the peripheral deposits around the side of the dustbin.

6. After 4-5 days' fermentation, the fermentation will slow down considerably and the beer must be siphoned into gallon jars, or an "Ex wine" 5 gallon polythene cube, leaving the heavy yeast deposit behind.

7. Fit airlocks to the gallon jars, or crack open the tap of the cube and insert a wad of cotton wood in the spout to stop bacteria getting in, and to allow the gases of secondary fermentation to escape.

8. Check the specific gravity of the beer regularly with a hydrometer and when it has stabilised (same reading between SG 8 and 12 for five days) the beer is ready for bottling or casking.

BOTTLING

1. Clean and sterilise the bottles, and add to each one a scant half teaspoonful of white sugar per pint.

2. Siphon the beer into the bottles, leaving ¾-1 in. airspace between the top of the beer and the underside of the stopper.

3. Fit the stoppers or crown caps as applicable, and store the bottles in a cool place where the temperature is around the 55-60°F mark.

4. Mature for three weeks before drinking.

CASKING

1. Clean and sterilise the barrel and add ½ ounce of white sugar per gallon of capacity.

2. Siphon in the beer and fill to within the bottom of the thread of the filler cap.

3. Replace the cap and injector unit, and leave the beer for a week to condition before sampling.

CHAPTER 4

Easy recipes

I have devised some really delicious beers: light ales, pale ales, bitters, stouts and even lager for you to try following the basic method described in the last chapter.

The hardest beer to make is the first one. There is nothing like actually brewing the beer to demonstrate how easy it is to make. Just reading the instructions will only make you thirsty, not knowledgeable!

By now you will have decided on what equipment to use for the mashing process; either a mashing boiler or a large dixie pan. Regardless of which method you choose, the following reasoning has been built into the brewing instructions.

Keep the temperature of the grain mix when mashing as near to but not exceeding 150°F especially during the first ten minutes or so.

By applying this simple theory you create the best conditions for enzymes (found naturally in malt) to complete the starch conversion process.

Really the performance of enzymes is like the behaviour of yeast during fermentation. Around 60-70°F the fermentation is perfect, below 40°F the yeast stops working and above 100°F the yeast will die. Mashing is best at 150°F and at the relative temperature extremes it will stop or die as well.

In the basic recipe you will recall that Gypsum and Epsom salts were used in the brewing water. All the light coloured beers require these salts and the dark beers a teaspoonful of chalk instead.

BEER

Recipe for 5 gallons
6 lb. Crushed pale malt
2 lb. White sugar
2½ ozs. Goldings hops
Beer yeast.

"AMBER ALE"

Recipe for 5 gallons of Bitter beer.
7 lb. Crushed pale malt
1 lb. Demerara sugar
1 Dessertspoonful of Gravy Browning
3½ oz. Goldings hops.
Beer yeast.

EASY LIGHT ALE

Recipe for 4 gallons
4½ lb. Crushed pale malt
1 lb. White sugar
2 oz. Cracked crystal malt
2 oz. Goldings hops
Beer yeast.

"CHARGER" Light Ale

Recipe for 5 gallons at a S.G. of 35
5 lb. Crushed pale malt
1 lb. Soft brown sugar
2 oz. Goldings hops
Lager beer yeast.

"PIPKIN" Pale Ale

Recipe for 5 gallons at a S.G. of 50
7 lb. Crushed pale malt
½ lb. Flaked rice
1½ lb. Invert sugar
3 oz. Goldings hops
1oz. Seedless Lager hops
Beer Yeast.

40

"REVIVAL" Pale Ale

Recipe for 5 gallons at a S.G. of 50
6 lb. Crushed pale malt
2 lb. Demerara sugar
4 oz. Cracked crystal malt
2 oz. Cracked wheat malt
3 oz. Goldings hops
Beer yeast.

"ROMSEY STOUT"

Recipe for 4 gallons at a S.G. of 50
7 lb. Crushed pale malt
9 oz. Roast barley
1½ oz. Fuggles hops
½ oz. Goldings or Northern Brewer hops
Stout yeast.

"MATCH"

Recipe for 5½ gallons of Mild Ale at a S.G. of 38
6 lb. Crushed pale malt
½ lb. Cracked roast barley
1 lb. Soft dark brown sugar
2 oz. Fuggles or Northern Brewer hops
Beer yeast.

HALLERTAU LAGER

Recipe for 4 gallons at a S.G. of 36
5 lb. Crushed pale malt
1½ oz. Hallertau hops
Lager yeast.

"BLACK BEAUTY"

Recipe for 4 gallons of Sweet Stout at a S.G. of 42
4½ lb. Crushed pale malt
½ lb. Cracked black malt
¼ lb. Cracked crystal malt
1 lb. White sugar
1 lb. Lactose
1 oz. Fuggles hops
½ oz. Northern Brewer hops
Beer yeast.

SPECIAL BROWN ALE

Recipe for 4 gallons at a S.G. of 42
5 lb. Crushed pale malt
½ lb. Flaked rice
¼ lb. Roast barley
¼ lb. Black malt
¾ lb. Lactose
1½ oz. Fuggles hops
Beer yeast.

CHAPTER 5

Other systems
of mashing

1. Floating mash-tun

THE two methods of mashing described in the basic procedure are simple and successful. Prior to using these techniques,
I devised a method of mashing especially for brewers
who have a large boiler, e.g. 5 gall. or 10 gall.
Burco. The system was based on floating an airtight polythene bucket in hot water in the boiler. By almost totally
immersing the mash-tun in a bulk of water at the right temperature for mashing, a heat sink was provided to maintain the "goods" temperature at the correct value. After
mashing, the boiler water could be used for sparging.

Diagram 1 on page 44 shows the arrangement.

The mash-tun is a 3 gallon polythene bucket fitted with
an air tight lid and tap. Being cheaper, it is naturally an
attractive proposition compared with other systems. If you
do decide on this type, make sure that the bucket can withstand the strenuous working conditions. Take into account
that the bucket has got to hold up to 20 lb. of hot grain and
water, and also withstand temperatures getting on for boiling
point. Thin walled buckets tend to flex when hot, resulting
in the loss of the airtight seal that renders the mash-tun useless
for this technique.

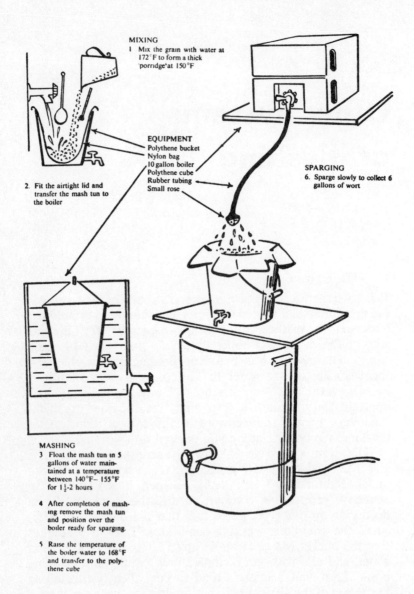

MIXING

1 Mix the grain with water at 172°F to form a thick 'porridge' at 150°F

EQUIPMENT
Polythene bucket
Nylon bag
10 gallon boiler
Polythene cube
Rubber tubing
Small rose

SPARGING

6. Sparge slowly to collect 6 gallons of wort

2. Fit the airtight lid and transfer the mash tun to the boiler

MASHING

3 Float the mash tun in 5 gallons of water maintained at a temperature between 140°F– 155°F for 1½-2 hours

4 After completion of mashing remove the mash tun and position over the boiler ready for sparging.

5 Raise the temperature of the boiler water to 168°F and transfer to the polythene cube

44

The grain needs to be retained in a large meshed nylon bag supported above the tap by some form of false bottom.

For really efficient mashing, this technique cannot be bettered. The only disadvantage is that the equipment takes slightly longer to set up than the boiler and dixie methods.

The following procedure is described using the ingredients for the five gallons of bitter made in the insulated food container example. (See page 34.) The basis of the recipe was 6 lb. of crushed pale malt and ½ lb. cracked crystal malt, and the modified technique is as follows:—

Mashing

1. Heat up at least five gallons of tap water to 172°F in a large boiler. If you are brewing in a medium or hard water area, water treatment should not be necessary. In soft water areas though, the addition of a level teaspoonful of Gypsum (BP Grade Plaster of Paris) and half a teaspoonful of Epsom Salt to the boiler water should benefit the mash reactions.

2. Evenly mix the Pale and Crystal Malts in a separate 2 gallon bucket. Line the inside of the mash-tun bucket with the nylon bag and fold the surplus mesh over the rim.

3. Place the mash tun beneath the tap of the boiler. Open the tap and allow the hot water to flow into the mash-tun. At the same time, scoop the crushed malt from the bucket into the mash-tun, stirring continuously to ensure that the mixture maintains a thick porridge like constituency. About one and a half gallons of water will be needed for the six and a half pounds of malt. The mixing should be carried out as quickly as possible to ensure an even distribution of heat that should result in the mean temperature of the grain and water settling out at 150°F. Any divergence from this target figure must be rectified as soon as possible by small additions of boiling or cold water. At the end of mixing the mashing water should just cover the surface of the grains.

4. Fold in the nylon bag, and replace the lid of the mash-tun checking that the seal is airtight.

5. The total weight of the mash-tun will be about 17 lb., and must obviously be treated with care and respect. Lift it into the boiler, where it should float in the remaining water. If, however, the mash-tun sinks due to the shape of the boiler, just add hot water to give sufficient buoyancy to raise it an inch or so from the boiler bottom. Suspend the thermometer in the boiler water and note the temperature.

6. Replace the boiler lid and switch off the heating supply. Drape a large towel over the boiler to conserve the heat.

7. Maintain the temperature of the boiler water between 165 and 145°F for 1½–2 hours. This is extremely easy, and I usually find that the water only needs boosting once during this period.

8. After one hour's mashing, remove the mash-tun from the boiler to check the progress of the reactions. Remove a teaspoonful of the grains and place on a white saucer. Add a few drops of iodine to the mixture and if there is no blue discolouration of the iodine, all the starch has been converted to malt sugars. Even after a satisfactory iodine test, the mash-tun must remain for another hour to allow a further breakdown of the malt sugars to ensure a well balanced wort.

9. Check the temperature of the mash at this stage and return to 150°F if necessary with boiling water. Fortunately any dilution of the mash after saccharification is actually beneficial to subsequent sugar breakdown processes.

10. Return the mash-tun to the boiler and continue mashing.

Sparging

1. After mashing remove the mash-tun and raise the boiler water temperature back to 172°F.

2. Transfer the five gallons or so of water to the poly-thene cube or plastic pressure barrel sparger. The remaining sparging procedure and the subsequent boiling, and fermentation process are the same as described for the basic method.

2 The Burco brewing boiler

On the market is a 5 gallon boiler, produced by Burco's and specifically designed for home brewing. It is basically a standard boiler that has been adapted for mashing grain. A perforated insert basket can be purchased with the boiler for holding the grain, and a pre-set, very accurate thermostat incorporated in the boiler will maintain the temperature of the mash to within a few degrees of 150°F. The arrangement works well, and excellent extraction rates can be achieved from the pale malt and adjuncts.

A slightly different approach is needed for the mashing process than for the techniques previously described in this book. The same theory applies in ensuring that the mash temperature starts at 150°F., with the grain and water forming a reasonably stiff mixture.

Method

As with the floating mash-tun method, to illustrate the procedure for mashing with the Burco mashing boiler, I will give the technique using the same ingredients as for the basic method, i.e. 6 lb. crushed pale malt and ½ lb. of crushed crystal malt.

Calibration for Mashing

First of all, the boiler must be calibrated to 150°F for mashing. Fill the boiler with three gallons of water and select the control switch to 4 (for boiling). Suspend a thermometer in the water. Stir the water before taking the temperature and when it reaches 150°F, turn the temperature control switch back to the left slowly until a click is heard. This means that the thermostat has cut off the heater and the temperature will start to fall. When the temperature has fallen a couple of degrees the thermostat will automatically switch on the heat again and the cycle of events will start again.

Leave the boiler to control the temperature for about a quarter of an hour to ensure that the mean setting has stabilised at 150°F. Note: the temperature will cycle a few degrees above and below the figure; this is perfectly all right for mashing.

The setting, which should be somewhere between positions 2 and 3 on the control switch, should be marked with a pencil for future reference.

It is a good idea to extend this procedure for 145°F and 155°F settings on the control switch dial as well.

Mashing

Fill the boiler with approximately three gallons of water, treated for bitter production. Replace and position the perforated insert basket in the boiler. The water around and inside the basket will level off due to the holes in the basket walls and bottom, and should be about four inches deep. Adjust the level if necessary to this figure by adding or removing water from the main boiler.

Suspend a brass tubed thermometer in the basket, replace the boiler lid, and switch on the heat. When the temperature reaches 162°F, select the control switch to the mash position. Stir in the mixture of dry grain into the water in the basket, and maintain stirring for about one minute. Check that the temperature is settling out to 150°F. Adjust with boiling or cold water, if necessary, to bring the temperature to within a degree of this figure. Test the mash acidity with pH paper and adjust as necessary as well.

Replace the lid on the boiler and leave the boiler to control the mashing process automatically. Confirm that starch end point has been passed sometime within the last hour of the 2–3 hour mash.

After mashing, open the tap and collect the first turbid worts in a large jug, and return them to the surface of the mashed grain. When the wort is running fairly bright from the tap, collect and transfer it to another container, such as a plastic dustbin.

Sparge the drained grain husks with another three gallons of hot water to retrieve the remaining extract. Actually, this sparging can be omitted by filling the boiler again with water sufficient for the grain to float, to enable the extract to be leached out instead of sparged. Switch on the boiler again and raise the water temperature up to about 170°F, stirring the goods occasionally to wash out the extract. After a five minute soak around 170°F, drain off the malt liquor.

Quite a lot of grain debris will be washed through when using this technique, which could be injurious to the quality of the beer. Thus if it is at all possible, allow the collected worts to settle for a few minutes and then rack it off the sediment into the boiler.

The boiling, fermentation, and all the other stages are the same as was detailed for the basic method.

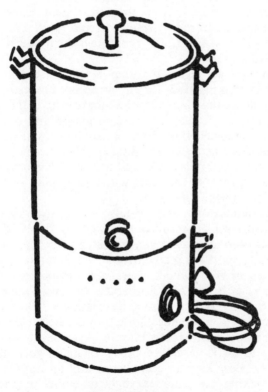

Burco Boiler

CHAPTER 6

Malt

Pale Malt

PALE MALT is the basis for all quality beers and should normally provide approximately three quarters of the fermentable extract. Beers brewed from this malt using mashing techniques are commonly referred to as 'grain' beer by home brewers to draw a distinction between them and those made from malt extract.

Some people regard mashing as being a completely new method of making beer for the amateur. From the birth of modern home-brewing about a decade ago, the centuries old techniques of mashing were forgotten and discarded as the craft welcomed the advent of malt extract syrups. The convenience of malt extract enabled the earlier home-brewers to bypass the complex malting and mashing processes and produce a drinkable beer that was cheap, quick to make and needed very little skill.

The limitations and disadvantages regarding quality and flavour were initially outweighed by these advantages, but it has been apparent over the latter years that the enthusiasm and support for malt extract beers is rapidly dwindling. More and more home-brewers are beginning to analyse their beers critically and appreciate that the restriction imposed by these syrups cannot be overcome. Beer kits have accelerated this viewpoint. Quite frankly, if you are prepared to accept and drink these inferior beers, on a purely convenience basis, it would be better to make your beer from beer kits. Beer kits are a far better and far more consistent way of making beer, and the slight difference in price makes messing about with malt extract not worthwhile.

Buying Malt

Pale Malt is available from most reputable home-brew stockists, who usually buy in bulk from the wholesalers or direct from the maltster, and package it down into smaller quantities for the amateur trade.

Quantities over the counter are usually in 1 lb., 7 lb., and 14 lb. packages or multiples thereof. Always try to purchase malt in the largest quantity your pocket and strength can handle! Dry malt grains have better keeping qualities than the liquid extracts, so there should be no worries about the grain going "off" during storage.

Never, however, purchase a large quantity from retail stockists without carrying out a trial brew with a small representative sample of the goods beforehand. Very little information is furnished with pale malt regarding extract potential and nitrogen content, and thus the only test apparatus we have got for malt analysis is our brewing gear, where the final appraisal is in the quality of the finished product!

A visual inspection of a sample of malt can give a useful pointer to provide a broad acceptance of its brewing quality. A sample handful should contain very little dust, debris and foreign matter. A high proportion of straw, fragments, rootlets and dust may indicate that the malt is left-over stock and from a doubtful source.

The malt grains themselves should be plump, an even size and shape, and possess a light straw coloured hue. Consistent appearance of each grain, coupled with these attributes, is a sign of good malting. Nice fat firm grains are good extract bearers, and an even size and shape are essential for correct crushing.

A sample grain should be easily crushed when squeezed between the thumb nail and finger to release its powdery interior. It should also be possible with good malt to write with it on a board using a half grain like a stick of chalk. Always check the interior, extract-bearing portion of the grain. Some grains, which are kilned too fast and at too high a temperature, look nice and fat, but are just ballooned by a large pocket of trapped air.

The barley malt grain is crammed with complex plant substances with chemical formulae as long as your arm! The exact nature of many of the organic substances is not known very well even in to-day's scientific world, and most are only identified by their action or effect on a chemical change. A brewer just needs a basic appreciation of these substances, and also how they can be manipulated to suit his particular brewing requirements.

The most important characteristic of malt is the extract potential which indicates the amount of fermentable sugar which can be produced from the grain. Good quality malt will yield four-fifths of its weight as sugar. The major proportion of this extract is derived from the starchy malt flour and also the cellulose products that surround and bind together each particle of grain.

The most reliable method of assessing the brewing quality is by measuring the nitrogen content. Although only usually constituting between 1.4 and 2.0 per cent of the corn, its presence is of paramount importance in brewing. The whole approach to the subsequent brewing processes can be delicately balanced on a knife edge over this minute percentage of matter. The difference between too little and too much nitrogen can be decided by as little as a tenth of one per cent. Embraced in this figure are many nitrogen based products such as proteins, nutrients and amino acids. Too high a nitrogen content can cause hazy beer and inadequate nitrogen can result in a deficiency of the yeast nutrient properties of the wort and lead to poor fermentations.

Some of the protein products add to the palate fullness of the beer and are instrumental in forming and retaining the head of the beer.

Consideration of the nitrogen products is a necessity in all stages of beermaking, since it has far reaching effects and fixes quite definitely the parameters for formulating recipes.

By careful formulations and sound brewing practices, problems arising from nitrogen content are not normally experienced.

The remaining one fifth of the grain is the non extract-forming matter that includes the husks, the embryo plant and ash, which have very little contribution to the subsequent processes.

CHAPTER 7

Coloured malts

NEARLY all types of beer derive some flavouring from roasted grain. Raw or malted cereals can be used for this purpose to provide an infinite variety of flavour for our beers. Proportions formulated into the grist are usually quite small due to their comparatively strong flavours. The roasted unmalted grains are solely for colour and flavour, wheareas the malted varieties can make some contribution to the fermentable extract and strength of the brew.

Crystal Malt

Crystal Malt, or Caramel Malt as it is known on the continent, is made from green malt. The malting process is interrupted after germination has succeeded in converting the barley starch to malt flour. Instead of drying this wet malt, the temperature in the ovens is raised to mashing heat so that each corn undergoes its own mashing process, thus converting the contents to sugars. The subsequent drying and kilning crystallises the sugars and tones the husk to a deep golden yellow colour.

This malt is easy to manage, presenting no problems of starch conversion, and is an ideal "body bui'der" for the sweeter types of beer.

Black Malt

Black Malt is a highly roasted malt made from kilned malt. Roasting is carried out in revolving drums at temperatures marginally below that which would carbonise the grain (about 450°F). In this intense heat, all the malt sugar caramelises to give the malt its renowned rich, luscious flavour.

Like coffee, it tastes far better when freshly roasted. If you feel adventurous and brave sometime when the wife is out of the kitchen, try experimenting by roasting pale malt grain in the oven set between 400 and 450°F. The grains should be nicely roasted approximately five minutes after the first billow of black choking smoke issues forth from the stove!

Roast Barley

Roast Barley is an excellent grain which has taken far too long to reach the counters of the amateur trade. It is drier and not so rich in flavour as Black Malt. For dry Stouts this grain cannot be surpassed, where it is claimed that it contributes to the firmness and whiteness in the head. I am all in favour of changing the emphasis in dark beers from Black Malt to this barley grain. It is an unmalted grain, roasted to a reddish brown colour. By omitting the malting process, theoretically it should be much cheaper.

Other roasted grains

Amber and Brown are little used nowadays since their qualities and attributes can be generally bettered by other malts.

Mild Ale Malt

Mild Ale Malt is malted barley roasted slightly more than Pale Malt. The higher kilning temperature tends to give a fuller flavoured beer and results in a darker coloured malt with a slightly restricted diastatic activity.

Roast Malt

Roast Malt is the malted equivalent of Roast Barley, and can be formulated as a direct substitute in most recipes. The slight contribution to the extract can be ignored for most practical purposes.

CHAPTER 8

Malt adjuncts

For centuries beer was made from just malt, hops, water and yeast. This happy state of affairs existed up to about sixty years ago, when the character of our beer was undergoing subtle changes. High gravity beers of excellent quality were brewed using the simple infusion mash system. About this time, too, great advances were being made in farming techniques. New ideas on fertilizers were implemented and the farmers returned bumper crops of high quality malting barley. Extract yields were increased by up to 20 per cent, which initially pleased the maltster and brewer.

Brewers then began to experience persistent hazes in their high gravity beers when using these improved barleys. The only way to re-establish the clarity was to reduce the quantity of malt used in the grist. Reducing the amount of fermentables produced a weaker beer, which brought about an immediate outcry from the ever-watchful beer drinkers. In those days, weak beer still could have twice as much alcohol as our best beer to-day, so I shudder to think of what those old-timers would have thought about our keg bitters!

Cane sugar was well known as a source for producing alcohol, but was never favoured since it tended to produce a thin bodied beer. The need for an alcohol producing source that could still contribute body became urgent. Experiments showed that other starch could be added to the mash-tun and be efficiently converted to sugar by the malted barley. Up to 20 per cent in the form of rice or maize could be utilised by this means.

The power of barley malt to convert extra starch was an extremely important discovery, and changed the whole attitude to brewing in this country. Taxes on malting barley accelerated the use of these economical adjuncts. Laws were passed permitting the use of these starch bearing products because it was appreciated that the equipment for the well established infusion mash systems could not be easily converted to cope with these new malts.

The offending constituent in the malt that caused this major upheaval was later determined to be the nitrogen content. Minor changes in this group of products can play havoc with the formulation of the grist.

On the continent, the decoction system of mashing could easily deal with high nitrogen malt, and for this reason, many countries banned adjuncts and sugar as being unnecessary additives to beer.

Malt adjuncts, then, are technologically desirable for our top fermenting beers made with the infusion system of mashing.

As mentioned before, Maize and Rice are the most common adjuncts. They cannot be used in the raw state, and must be boiled to gelatinise the starch before they can be accepted by the mash reactions. Grits, as they are referred to, are rolled into thin "flakes" after the cooking process. It is far better for amateurs to use unmalted adjuncts in the latter form.

Flaked Rice

Flaked rice is a readily available product and can be purchased at most grocery stores. It is probably the most useful flaked adjunct on account of its low colour and flavouring properties. These attributes make it an extremely useful ingredient for the light coloured beers, especially high gravity Pale Ales. Dilution of the nitrogen content means that high alcohol beers can be produced without the fear of poor clarity.

56

Flaked Maize

Flaked Maize has all the advantages of the Flaked Rice and will also contribute flavour. The "corn" taste is quite acceptable, but it is generally more suited to the sweeter dark beers and lagers than to the drier Pale Ales. It is, however, one of the best adjuncts to use for full bodied bitters.

Flaked Barley

These flakes impart a lovely "grainy" flavour to the beer and are consequently regarded as the best flaked adjunct in this respect.

More attention needs to be paid to the quality of these flakes than the Pale Malted Barley. Judicial selection is extremely important commercially on account of its protein stability. I appreciate that we have no chance at our end of the trade to carry out tests, but it is useful to know that problems can exist with this flake. Barley is the only cereal to contain beta globulin, a haze-forming protein not present in the other adjuncts. Hence the inclusion of Flaked Barley will tend to increase the risk of haze.

Barley, though, is far richer in water soluble gums than other cereals, and thus can provide a useful service in maintaining the head retention properties of the beer. In the darker beers, especially Stouts, where haze problems are no worry, Flaked Barley is unsurpassed as an adjunct for flavour and head retention.

In the lighter beers, the inclusion of up to one ounce per gallon of the flakes should cause very little problem, and indeed will offer many benefits.

Malt Extract

Malt Extracts are simply concentrated worts. The popular makes on the home-brewing scene are made from the worts of lightly cured malts, concentrated in vacuum evaporators at low temperatures to preserve the diastatic activity.

The method of manufacture produces a highly fermentable syrup containing about 80 per cent solids. In preserving the enzyme activity, many desireable features of a well balanced wort are lost. Beers are made using these syrups as the base ingredient, but rarely can they match the quality of an "all grain" beer.

Malt Extract is a difficult substance to classify. It ferments out to zero gravity like sugar, but leaves the malty flavour of grain in the beer. Some types leave a characteristic tang of caramel which I regard as being quite objectionable.

For brewers with limited brewing capacity, these extracts could prove an advantage on the grounds of convenience and could be formulated into the mashing techniques. Obviously, one would have to experiment to arrive at a satisfactory balance between quality and convenience.

My tests have shown that the diastatic activity is about on a par with Pale Malt grains. Diastatic activity, as measured on the Linter Scale, is about 40-60 for both malts. Being a syrup, with temperature sensitive enzymes, creates difficulties in calculating mash temperature parameters (e.g. strike heat temperature). Consequently, I rarely use it for mash-tun conversion. In the copper it makes an ideal adjunct for supplementing the fermentables in a dark beer wort.

Torrefied Barley

Torrefied Barley is a useful ingredient on account of its mechanical properties which influence the efficiency of mashing and sparging. It is a very large grain made by heating barley in an oven until it "pops" like the breakfast cereal "Puffed Wheat". It gives porosity to the mashed grain during sparging, preventing set mashes and creating conditions for maximum wort extraction.

From experience, I have found that too high a proportion of this cereal can leave a "woody" taste in the beer. Amounts should be kept below 5 per cent, except for Mild Ales, which can benefit from up to twice this figure.

Oats

Oats are rarely used nowadays. The exception is in Oatmeal Stouts, where its inclusion is mainly for nutritional reasons rather than flavour. Oats contain a high percentage of oils which adversely affect the head retention properties of beer.

58

Wheat Malt

Wheat is a difficult cereal to malt because the acrospire, or shoot, is very susceptible to damage and disease.

A few ounces of this malt in a brew impart a pleasant grain flavour and fullness, and also seem to assist with the foaming properties of the beer.

The nitrogen content may be very much higher than Barley Malt and must therefore be considered when formulating recipes.

Wheat Syrup

Wheat Syrup is just a malt extract made from malted wheat rather than Barley. It can be used to replace wheat malt grains and has the advantage that it does not need mashing. Consequently, it could be used to contribute up to 15 per cent of the grist.

Brewing Flour

There are several specialised wheat flour adjunct available on the amateur market. Their main attribute is to act as diluents to high nitrogen malts with the benefit of maintaining, at the same time, the body and fullness of the beer. The flavour is slight and unobtrusive, which makes these adjuncts ideal partners for Lager malts where the delicate hop flavours must be unaltered in the finished beer.

The big disadvantage is that the flour increases the tendency to restrict the porosity of the "goods" during mashing that can result in set mashes and flooding during the sparging process.

CHAPTER 9

Sugar

SUGAR can be classed as a malt adjunct. It contributes alcohol and strength to the brew without distracting too much from the flavour of the malts.

Sound technological reasons can be put forward to demand the inclusion of this economic adjunct. Too large a proportion, though, will inevitably lead to thin and poorly balanced beers.

Sugar is devoid of nitrogenous matter and thus its inclusion will produce a beer that will mature more quickly than beer made with malt alone. High gravity beers can be brewed without fears on the clarity of the finished beer.

White Sugar

Common household white sugar (sucrose) is our cheapest and most readily available fermentable carbohydrate. It is produced from refined sugar cane or sugar beet and other sources, and is sold under many guises. Granulated, Cube, Icing and Castor Sugars are chemically identical; the only difference being the texture and the price. Consequently, the cheapest, Granulated Sugar, should be used in any recipe calling for this adjunct. Refined sugar is a very pure product and can be assumed to be 100 per cent fermentable. Commercially, it is rarely used in brewing because the refining process increases the cost and removes some of the desirable "impurities" that enhance flavour.

Invert Sugar

Invert Sugar is made by boiling ordinary sugar in a dilute solution of acid, and gains its name through its ability to change the direction of light after this process. Ready made invert sugar comes in the form of a crystalline mass containing approximately 20 per cent water and due allowance must be made for this point in formulating recipes.

From a chemical standpoint, this sugar is the best for brewing, since it is immediately fermentable by yeast.

White sugar must first be "inverted" by the enzyme invertase in yeast before the fermentation can commence, but in practice, I have never been able to detect any time lag in fermentation that could positively be attributed to this cause.

Home-made invert sugar can be made by boiling 2 lb. of white sugar in one pint of water with one teaspoonful of citric acid, until the solution has a pale golden colour. The acidity must be neutralised afterwards with chalk to increase the pH value back to 7.0. If this is not carried out, the delicate balance of acidity will be upset that will increase the chances of the beer "souring" during maturation. The effect on flavour and colour in the presence of chalk must also be considered for light beer brews.

Glucose Chips

Glucose Chips are manufactured by the acid conversion of purified maize starch. The large chips of crystalline sugars contain about 10 per cent water and tend to produce a much drier flavoured beer than either cane or invert sugars. The cost is approximately double that of household sugar, so that the merits of flavour must justify the extra expenditure to warrant its place in your brewing store. No doubt, a few experiments will consolidate your views.

Dark Sugars

Under this heading come all the partially refined Cane Sugars. Demerara, Soft Brown, Light Brown, and Barbados, can all be usefully employed in brewing. Again, they cost more than white sugar, but I consider that the luscious flavour of these darker varieties well worth the investment. Moisture and colouring matter reduce the extract potential by a few percent.

Lactose

Lactose or Milk Sugar, is unfermentable by brewery yeasts and is used to maintain a degree of sweetness in darker beers. That old time favourite, Milk Stout, owes its name to this sweetener. The lower grades are very susceptible to defects and off flavours, and must therefore be purchased with reserved caution. Some contain unwanted milk derivatives that destroy the foaming properties of beer. Tasting a sample of the dry sugary powder will readily reveal any undue cheesy flavour. The degree of sweetness is not so intense as that of household sugar, so proportionately more is needed in the brew.

The use of lactose is the lesser of evils. The flavour is similar to saccharine and is not so compatible as a sweetening agent as white sugar. It does not blend, or marry, with the sugars derived from malt and thus it can always be detected in the beer.

Specialised brewing sugars are available commercially where the fermentability can be altered to suit the brewer's requirements. These are based on starch sugars, not lactose, and as such, they are a far better proposition for flavouring. The brewer can also choose the colour of sugar for subsequent tinting of the finished beer.

Lactose is not entirely unfermentable. Certain wild yeasts have the ability to reproduce in the presence of this sugar, and special attention must be paid to sterilisation to prevent contamination, burst bottles. etc.

Artificial Sweeteners

Low calorie artificial sweeteners are generally not very acceptable in beermaking. Although they are non-fermentable, chemical breakdown progresses between the saccharine matter and the acids of the beer, which after a few days, changes the sweetness to an intense bitterness. Some brands, particularly "Sweetex Liquid" do not display this fault so readily and can be used with advantage in some quick maturing beers.

Caramels

Caramel is the name given to sugar that has been heated in the presence of acids, alkalies, and ammonium salts, to form a soluble brown, bitter substance tasting of burnt sugar.

Its prime use in beermaking is as a colouring agent. Good caramel should possess highly concentrated colouring matter so that the amount added to shade a beer will not affect its flavour. To ensure stability of the colouring, caramel should always be added prior to, or even during the boiling of the wort.

Specially prepared solutions are sold by most home-brew stockists, or alternatively suitable brands of gravy browning may be used. Check the contents label of the latter to see that it does not contain salt, or any other ingredient bar the caramel solution. Approximately one teaspoonful of the neat solution will change the colour of one gallon of water to that expected of a bitter beer.

Treacles and syrups

These are viscous solutions of unrefined or partially refined sugars. Black treacle, Golden Syrup and Molasses are the most common known types. Their role in beermaking is rather limited due to indeterminable characteristics of unrefined compounds which can sometimes adversely affect the clarity of the brew. In minute doses, the strong residual flavour could be usefully employed to take the edge off the purity in household sugars. My recipes mostly favour brown sugars in preference to white for this reason. Experiments with 1–2 ounce doses of these sugars in a brew could possibly cultivate some interesting flavours.

Liquorice

Liquorice is a black substance manufactured from a root herb that possess a very distinct characteristic taste and aroma. The thick black oily sticks can be dissolved and used to give a depth of flavour to certain medicinal stouts.

Honey

Honey is the oldest form of sugar known to man, and was used extensively in many of the early fermentable beverages, such as mead, old ales and herbal beers. Other forms of sugar are now more readily available, more economical, and impart a better and consistent flavour than honey, so that its contribution to brewing can be virtually ignored.

CHAPTER 10

Hops

HOPS have been used to flavour beers in Europe since the early 1400's. Other herbs and extracts had been tried prior to this era to complement the sweetness of these fermented malt liquors with various degrees of success.

The introduction of hops to England by traders from Flanders caused a major upheaval in the thinking on ale brewing. Initially the hop was regarded as being a "noxious weed". Prejudice and opposition were so intense that the poor humble plant was banned for brewing purposes for certain periods by the law of the land. Arguments over its merits raged and echoed over the centuries. Gradually the opposition diminished as its superior medicinal and preservative properties became recognised.

Nowadays, the characteristic bitterness is so much a part of beer that it is included now principally for reasons of flavour.

Hop plant

The hop plant is a spindly weed botanically related to the Cannabis-producing drug, hemp or wort, hence the use of the word "wort" in connection with brewing. Calling the plant a "hop" is too easy for Botanists, who prefer to confuse our simple lives and categorise it as "Humulus lupulus".

The plant is perennial, producing a fresh bine annually, which may grow up to about 30 ft. in length, coiling clockwise upward and around any adjacent supports. It is dioecious, meaning that the male and female flower grow on separate plants. Fertilisation is effected by air borne pollen in an extremely efficient manner. One male plant can fertilise about five hundred female plants. Prowess in the reproduction stakes of the male is currently thwarting the experiments to grow seedling hops in this country. Identifying and elimina-

ting all male plants, including any wild ones, is proving a mammoth task.

It is only the cone-shaped female flowers that are used in beermaking. The male flowers are very small, $\frac{1}{4}$ in. across, with five open petals, and grow in clusters. After the plant has flowered and produced its crop the bine is cut down, leaving the roots to produce next year's bine. Different varieties are suited to different climatic conditions and soils. For instance, the drier seasons tend to be better for the Golding type of hop, and wetter seasons for the Fuggle.

Hops are harvested usually within a day or two from 6th September. The strings are cut down or unhooked at the top, after which the cones are picked off and loaded into bins. Mechanical picking of hops is becoming increasingly popular in this country. Unfortunately, our traditional hops, the Goldings and Fuggles, do not lend themselves readily to machine picking, and in some areas they are being replaced with sturdier stock capable of withstanding the rough handling of these machines.

The hops are then sent to oast houses for drying and curing. In the green state they would quickly deteriorate and become useless for brewing purposes. Drying over the oast house fires stabilises their active constituents and also develops in them the most attractive flavour. The temperature and speed of drying has a major influence on the subsequent quality and brewing value of the hop.

From experience and analytical tests, slow drying over a period of 12 hours around "mashing" temperatures (140–150°F) seem to bring out the best qualities in most hops.

Wild hops

Around the country lanes near where I live, every year there is an abundance of wild hops growing in the hedgerows. These beautiful ripe hops became too much of a temptation, and a few years back I decided to try my hand at drying and curing. A couple of hours picking one Sunday afternoon produced two large dustbins filled with these wild hops, which I estimated to be sufficient to see me through the coming brewing year.

I dried the hops in a perforated tea chest, using my wife's hairdryer and hood attachment adapted to provide a steady current of hot air through the green hops. After half a day of this treatment, the dried hops were packaged and weighed. Much to my dismay, the bulk had been reduced in weight to yield only two pounds. The first two brews made with these hops were excellent for flavour, but subsequent beers were well below standard. My curing process obviously lacked the finesse of the Kentish oast houses, so I discarded the remainder of the batch.

Packaging

After drying and curing, the hops are packaged into large cylindrical cloth sacks called "pockets". Each is about 6–7 ft.

in length and about 2 ft. in diameter, and contains approximately 1½ cwts. of hops.

I am convinced that this cumbersome package was designed to foil the single handed attempts of some unscrupulous home-brewers, who would be delighted to whisk away the fruits of the Kent harvest!

Constituents of hops

As regards brewing value, the most important constituents of hops are:—

1. Resins
2. The essential oils
3. Tannins.

The resins are sub divided into hard and soft resins, based on their solubility in light petroleum spirit. Hard resins are ignored as they contribute nothing to the brewing value.

It is the soft resins, by virtue of their flavouring and preservative properties, that are of paramount importance to brewing. In turn, these can be again split into two fractions:—

1. Humulon (alpha acid) which contributes the major proportion of the bittering power and the antiseptic properties of the hop. Great attention is paid to this resin derivative in the commercial field, and hop samples are invariably analysed and quoted in terms of the alpha acid content. Alpha Acid is the best indication of the bittering power of the hop.

2. Lupulon (Beta acid), although present in greater quantities than the alpha constituent, has only about a tenth of the bittering power and is only a third as effective as a preservative.

Modern analytical techniques for hop quality ignore the beta resin content, and just concentrate on the determination of the alpha acid.

Typical constituents of a dried hop:—

Constituent	Percentage weight of cone
Alpha acid (Humulon)	7
Beta acid (Lupulon)	10
Hard resins	3
Essential oils	0.3
Tannin	3
Pectins	10
Seeds	25
Ash	10
Nitrogen	4
Sugars	3
Moisture	12
Diastase	Slight activity

The essential oils are responsible to a large extent for the characteristic aroma of hops, and thus are an important aspect in brewing value. About 90 per cent of the fragrant properties are lost when the hops are boiled in wort. Dry hopping in the post fermentation period can, however, offset this loss to a certain extent.

The tannins are an ill-defined group of substances that are recognised by their physical properties and characteristics rather than their chemical make-up. They have an astringent flavour and are readily soluble in hot water where they display the ability to precipitate protein matter. The latter reaction plays an important part in the behaviour of hops during copper boiling. The tannin, which is derived from the strigs and petals, combines with, and removes by precipitation, the haze-forming proteins of the wort.

Hops also contain a small percentage of soluble nitrogen, a useful source of yeast food.

Buying hops

On a cost per weight basis, hops are one of the most expensive ingredients in beermaking. Having confidence in the value of the hop before parting with your money can be quite hard to attain. Buying and grading hops takes many years of experience to become an expert. The time and involvement necessary can rarely be afforded by the amateur brewer, but common sense and a basic knowledge of what the expert looks for in a hop can go a long way in enabling us to make a reasonable judgement.

Home-brewing is now making significant inroads into the commercial market on brewing ingredients, and we can now compete and demand the very best quality materials. No longer should we accept the rejects and "left overs" after the commercial combines have taken their pickings. The latest season's hops should be readily available to all home brewers. Two reputable sources of supply are available to the amateur:—

1. Home brew shops
2. Direct from the hop merchants.

Most home brewers buy their hops together and other requisites from the first source. For convenience, reputable dealers stock several varieties often of the current seasons stock, packaged down into small quantities to suit our needs. Whole pockets are purchased by larger retailers in an endeavour to supply the very best to customers. The care taken by your stockist in reducing these bulk quantities down to manageable units can have an important influence on the subsequent brewing value of these hops.

Small quantities should preferably be sealed in airtight, clear polythene bags and the hops compressed again as far as practicable. The bag should then be wrapped again with brown paper to exclude sunlight, and the package shelved in a cool place.

I would strongly advise against buying hops that are dispensed loose from an open-topped plastic dustbin. For a few coppers extra, it pays to choose named varieties from the current season.

It is just not practical or economical for the retailer to allow direct hand sampling of the hop, and indeed it would be grossly unfair to demand such a test.

This is where polythene bags are a particularly useful safeguard in allowing a visual appraisal of the contents. Poor hops can be detected without ever actually touching or smelling them. Excessive fragmentation and debris from the hop cone is usually a sign of bad handling.

The quantity of seeds, leaves and foreign matter can easily be appraised. Old hops, and in particular those exposed to the atmosphere for long periods, become brittle and lose their "bounce" and silky sheen.

Good hops will spring back into shape when the bag is squeezed and released, and will generally look good.

As long as you are prepared to purchase a reasonable quantity, say 5-10 lbs., of a particular variety, then it is usually cheaper to buy direct from the Hop Merchants in London. The savings and the quality of the produce make it an attractive proposition for friends, or your club, to contribute to making up these quantities. New season's hops are put on to the market around the end of January following the previous year's autumn harvest.

The hop merchants are the experts and their advice on selection should be heeded. Be sensible over buying, and remember that if you ask for four ounces of Golding in the middle of the busy selling period, you will certainly get some advice!

You can be assured that the hops supplied by the merchants will be of the highest quality, and managed correctly to ensure that you will receive them in the peak of condition.

Storing hops

The best method for storage at home is to divide the batch into 1 lb. packs sealed in polythene bags. Each pack should be suitably labelled and stored in a cool dark place. Deterioration of hops can be very rapid if not stored in the right environment. Oxidation and the action of microscopic bacteria can ruin the brewing value in a short space of time. The latter effect can be minimised by storing the hops in a deep freezer or a refrigerator.

Examination of hops

Unless other data is available, physical appraisal of hops is, in our case, the only way of pre-judging the worth of a sample. Maybe in years to come, the variety, year and alpha acid content will accompany each sample, but I think it is wishful thinking on my part.

Fully ripe hops should always be our goal. Maturity can be indicated fairly accurately by the colour change. Young hops are a darker green, changing to a ligher shade when ripe and finally turning to a reddish brown when over ripe. The degree of colour will depend largely on the particular variety. Goldings have primrose-yellow tips on the petals when ripe, whereas the higher alpha content types tend to be a much darker colour all over.

Some brownish discolouration may be present after a wet season which can be difficult to distinguish from disease. Outer bract discolouration is only usually due to rain or wind damage. Disease shows itself by rotting and dark colouring on the strig.

Reddish brown spots on the petals may be the after effects of mould or Downy Mildew disease.

Pressing down the palm of the hand on the sample should show the elasticity or spring of the hop. Brittle cones, or strobiles, fragment under pressure, and malleable ones indicate dampness in the sample.

When judging, I like to remove a single cone and isolate one of the seeds. By rubbing off the frail outer coat, the actual seed underneath should be bright purple. Traces and patches of white are a sign of an unripe specimen.

Inspection of the base of the bracteole will show it to be covered with a light sulphur coloured, sticky powder called lupulin. This is the most important ingredient of the hop and it contains all the essential oils and resins. Attached to the bracteoles are numerous pollen-like grains which secrete the lupulin and form blister-like cells under the outer skin of the petal. When touched, the delicate skin bursts, releasing its oily contents and delightful "hop bouquet". The amount of this powder, known as "condition" or "fat", is visually appraised in determining the brewing quality. High alpha hops tend to produce more condition than the traditional varieties.

The final test of physical examination is the "rub". A portion of the hops is rubbed between the hand to disintegrate the sample. The oil resinous substance will stick to the palms of the hand and the broken petals should sift freely through the fingers. Heat generated by the rubbing action with warm hands assists in the release of aromatic esters from the hop oils. Cupping the hands and inhaling the bouquet will reveal quite a lot about the character of the hop. Even the coarser varieties have a pleasing "dry" aroma. Poor hops, regardless of variety, either possess very little aroma at all, or else a strong reek, slightly reminiscent of wet leaves.

The hop industry

For centuries, brewing has been an art relying on the skills of experienced experts. The advance of science and technology has, in the case of hops, created a demand to value by analytical techniques as well as by hand appraisal. Coupled with the increase in mechanisation of hop picking, and the ever present problems of disease, the poor hop has been in for a rough ride lately. Even so, this humble little plant has defied most of the attempts to embrace it with the advances of modern technology.

Despite vast research, the scientists still cannot isolate any ingredient or property of the hop that could be used as a measure of flavour. The nearest they can get is to determine the bitterness, which as you can appreciate, is only part of the story. For the darker beers, where hop flavour is substantially overshadowed by other factors, brewing to a set level of bitterness would seem a reasonable proposition.

The hop is rather an awkward commodity to handle and any means of reducing the bulk would also be a move in the right direction. Ideally, it would be nice to have just one hop cone with the equivalent bittering power of say, one pound of conventional hops. This will never be achieved, but considerable research has resulted in successfully producing hops with much more bitterness than the traditional Goldings and Fuggles varieties.

Mass produced beers nowadays demand consistency. By choosing and selecting hops to an alpha acid basis can effectively produce the same level of bitterness brew after brew. Initially this approach was reserved for dark beers, but now, brewing to alpha acid content has spread to the lighter type of beers, especially keg bitters.

Commercially, high alpha hops have many advantages. So important is this constituent that hop prices are largely pegged to this analysis, which tends to encourage the growers to forsake the old low acid varieties. Secondly, these new varieties are more resistant to the diseases that scour our fields, and consequently, are more economic due to less wastage.

Downy Mildew and Verticillium Wilt are becoming increasingly more embarrassing for the low alpha flavour hops such as the Goldings and Fuggles.

The first varieties bred for increased alpha acid did show more resistance to these diseases. Unfortunately, the increased bitterness was accompanied by poor, and in some cases objectionable, flavouring properties.

It seems likely that the problems of disease may soon be reduced to an acceptable level, and research is now being channelled into breeding high alpha content hops of good flavour.

The Goldings variety will be with us for many years to come, purely due to its superior flavouring properties. The brewers have found that their customers will shun beers brewed solely to alpha acid considerations that take no account of flavour.

I have purposely discussed some of the policies and commercial aspects of hop growing and marketing so that you can draw your own conclusions. What is good for the commercial trade is not necessarily good for us. If the big breweries had decided to return to brewing high quality beer to traditional flavours, then probably I would not be writing this book, or you reading it!

The fancy prices being asked for some of the new varieties is far in excess of their worth for our full flavoured beer.

Comparison of hops		*1972*
	Alpha acid	*per cent*
English varieties	*range per cent*	*crop*
Goldings,	3·5–5·0	
Early Bird		5
Eastwell		5
Cobbs		4
Mathon		1
Whitbread Golding Variety		
(W.G.V.)	4·5–5·5	10
Fuggles	3·5–4·3	35
Progress	4·0–5·3	3
Bullion	4·0–9·0	9
Bramling Cross (OT48)	5·2–6·0	16
Northern Brewer	6·0–8·0	6
Keyworth Mid Season (OR55)	6·0–7·5	3
New varieties		4
		100

	Alpha acid
Foreigh hops (seedless)	*range per cent*
Saaz	6·0–8·5
Hallertau	7·0–9·0
Hallertau—Northern Brewer	9·0–11·0
Styrian Goldings	6·0–8·5
B.C. Goldings	6·0–8·0

TYPES OF HOPS
Goldings

The original plant was selected from the Canterbury Hop Garden by a Mr. Golding about two hundred years ago, and represents the very best in English hops. It no longer exists as a pure strain and the name really refers to a number of related varieties. Early Bird, Eastwell, Cobbs and Mathons are currently the most popular varieties in this group.

They are a comparatively small hop with rounded compact cones barely ¾ in. long and with distinctive yellow-tipped petals. The colour of the cones is also a very much lighter shade of green than other varieties, and thus makes them easily recognisable. From my experience, the lighter the colour of English hops, the better the flavouring properties. The aroma is delicate, which makes the variety admirably suited for dry hopping. As a copper hop, it is unsurpassed for the production of high class Pale Ales and Bitters.

Commercially, top class Goldings command high prices completely out of context with their alpha acid content.

They yield very small crops per acre, and would certainly have been phased out through economic pressures if another hop could have been found to match their flavour and aroma. Resistance to disease is poor and the seed content rather high.

Whitbread Golding Variety (W.G.V.'s)

A very popular hop with a reasonable flavour, aroma and acid content coupled with disease resistance, especially Verticillium Wilt. I regard the flavour as being something like a cross between a Golding and a Fuggle. It is thus a very versatile hop, and it seems to partially bridge the gap between the traditional flavour varieties and the high acid types.

Fuggles

Fuggles are the mainstock of the English crop, commanding over a third of the total acreage. An economical hop, rather coarser in flavour than the Golding, but a heavy cropper, rich in lupulin, making it a favourite as a copper hop. The cones are dark green, square in section and pointed, and approximately twice the size of the Golding.

It is not very resistant to disease, nor particularly good for mechanical picking. In future, the acreage allocated to the Fuggle will almost certainly fall dramatically in favour of the newer, high alpha varieties.

Progress

Grown as a Fuggles replacement and now returning to popularity. Next to the Golding, this is my favourite hop. It has a beautiful aroma, good flavour and when used with best Kent Goldings, produces the best hop flavoured beer that I have ever tasted. Deserves far more recognition.

Bullion

One of the first high alpha varieties and displays very distinctive qualities, making it probably one of the easiest hops to identify. A side cut from a sample shows that the cones have retained their shape even under compression in the pocket. Individual cones are easily identifiable. The "nutty" appearance in sample is peculiar only to this variety. The aroma is very strong from a "rubbed" sample, which I personally find quite pleasant.

When used in beer it changes completely and imparts unusual taste and aroma, somewhat reminiscent of blackcurrants which is distinct, and really quite alien from other English hops. The alpha acid can be extremely high, reaching 9·0 per cent in a good year. From a grower's point of view it can be a gamble since the alpha acid content is very inconsistent, dipping as low as 4·0 per cent at times. This hop must never be used exclusively in a brew; the flavour is far too strong. In dark, heavy-bodied beers it can be formulated to provide up to about half the bitterness. Treated with caution, it can even be used in bitters. Adding a small handful to a five gallon boil can bring out interesting, pleasing flavour to a bitter. Bullion can often be detected in many commercial keg bitters.

Bramling Cross

Cyphered OT48, this crossbreed Golding variety can command an acreage equal to all other Goldings put together. It is one of the easiest hops to grow and manage. This hop should be reserved for the very best Bitters and Pale Ales. It is a perfect match for the sweeter, full-bodied draught beers and is excellent for dry hopping.

Northern Brewer

Economically, this hop is ideal for using with all dark beers. Good flavour and high alpha acid content have made it a brewer's favourite.

Northern Brewer often looks a poor, low grade hop, and without knowing its attributes, the average home brewer might be tempted to ignore it. Samples can sometimes look quite scruffy, with ill formed cones having a more reddish brown colouring than green. Usually its brewing value is not affected by these visual defects.

Keyworth Mid Season

A half brother of the Bullion, Keyworths Mid Season Cyphered OR55, is a good high alpha hop used extensively in heavy bodied dry stouts.

New varieties

Very little is known at present on the performance of new varieties. Generally, they have been selected as being resistant to the hop diseases, together with a high alpha acid content without the objectionable characteristics of the Bullion type of hop.

Continental hops

Continental hops are usually seedless, producing small and more compact cones than our English varieties. Seeds contribute nothing to the brewing value of the hops and can be regarded as redundant weight. Alpha acid content is quoted on the percentage of the total weight of the cone. Thus continental hops, without the handicap of seed weight, can quote alpha acid figures approximately a third higher than our own varieties, which can be rather misleading when assessing brewing value.

Saaz

The hops of Bohemia, in particular the Saaz, are world famous for their quality. This outstanding variety, an early red bine, is not a very heavy cropper, but produces the most sought after and choicest quality hop for the very pale, Pilsner type Lagers. On the home-brew scene, it is still a very scarce variety, demanding top prices.

Hallertau

Another of my favourite hops, coming from the famous hop growing district of the same name, north of Munich.

The plain Hallertau hop is sometimes referred to as the "low alpha" Hallertau. The cones are very firm, a dark green colour, with coarse-textured bracts. Because it is a continental hop, many home-brewers seem afraid to use it in any brew other than a Lager. This is absolute nonsense. In fact I have recently been using it as a copper hop replacement for all my recipes that previously called for Fuggles. The flavour and aroma are far superior, and now this variety is accounting for about a third of my total consumption of hops.

Hallertau Northern Brewer

This hop is just Northern Brewer grown seedless on the continental fields. It has the advantage of having a very strong preservative power and excellent flavour without carrying useless seeds.

Styrian Goldings

I gather that this hop was originally cultivated from English stock and is not really a Golding but is more characteristic of a Fuggle. An expensive hop which should be reserved for the best Pale Ales and Bitters.

North American hops
British Columbian hops

Many English varieties or derivatives are grown in North America and are imported to the country at times. Quite frankly, I was surprised to see them available at our end of the trade. The only ones that I have tried were the

B.C. Seedless Goldings which I found to be excellent value for money.

Hop rates

It is very difficult to make hard and fast rules regarding hop rates, because there are so many variables that need to be taken into consideration. The quality of the hops, the variety, season, the type of beer being brewed, its gravity and the characteristics of the brewing water must all be taken into account.

The information listed on the Hop Utilisation Summary Table is a guide to the particular requirements based on my personal judgement and preferences. Most of it is based on accepted practice, but you can be sure that it will not suit your particular palate in all cases. This is the beauty of home-brewing; you alter the ingredients to your own satisfaction.

The range of hop rates is a reflection of the differences in the starting gravities of the various types of beer. The column listing the rates in terms of ounces per gallon is self explanatory, but the Alpha Acid Units figure will bound to be a little confusing at first.

In the previous discussions, I explained how the bitterness of the hop was due to the alpha acid content, and how the brewing value and price were commercially pegged to this constituent. Gradually, more and more hops will be supplied to the amateur trade with a stated alpha acid content. Consequently, a need arises to digest and understand the implications of the acid content, and decide how it can be channelled to the best use for consistent quality control of our ales.

Brewing to alpha acid content

When I was first faced with the good fortune of having a sample of hops with quoted alpha acid figures, I was completely lost as to how to make the best use of this information. Out of necessity, I devised the following system to suit our amateur needs.

The alpha acid content is quoted as a percentage of the weight of the hop cones, and seeing that we usually work in terms of ounces rather than pounds, this was taken as the basis of my interpretation.

80

HOP UTILISATION SUMMARY TABLE

Hop rate/gallon   Preferred vaieties (maximum per cent of total)

Type	Starting gravity range	ounces (ozs)	Alpha Acid Units (A.A.U's)	First	%	Second	%	Third	%
Barley Wine	60–80	1·0 –1·4	5·0–7·0	Goldings	100	Hallertau	70	Progress	30
Pale Ale	40–55	0·6 –1·0	3·0–5·0	Goldings	100	Hallertau	60	OT48	25
Light Ale	30–40	0·4 –0·6	2·0–3·0	Goldings	100	OT48/ W.G.V.	30	Hallertau	30
Lager	30–45	0·25–0·40	1·3–2·0	Saaz	100	Hallertau	100	Other seed-less hops	100
Bitter	30–50	0·5 –0·7	2·5–3·5	Goldings	80	OT48/ W.G.V.	30	Progress	70
Mild ale	30–40	0·4 –0·5	2·0–2·5	Fuggles	100	Northern Brewer	70	Progress	70
Brown ale	35–45	0·4 –0·6	2·0–3·0	Northern Brewer	80	Fuggles	80	OR55	60
Sweet stout	35–45	0·5 –0·6	2·5–3·0	Northern Brewer	70	Fuggles	70	OR55	50
Dry stout	40–50	0·7 –1·0	3·5–5·0	OR55	60	Bullion	40	Northern Brewer	80

The units are Alpha Acid Units (A.A.U.'s)

One Alpha Acid Unit is represented by 1 per cent of acid in 1 ounce of hops. Thus, a hop having a quoted alpha acid content of 7 per cent will contribute 7 Alpha Acid Units for every ounce of hops. Two ounces of these hops will yield 14 A.A.U.'s and so on. The practical implications are demonstrated adequately by the following example.

A 4 gallon batch of best bitter is to be brewed to a bitterness equivalent to 3·0 A.A.U.'s per gallon, using two thirds Golding Hops and a third Progress Hops. The quoted alpha acid contents are 4·0 and 5·0 respectively for the 2 hops.

Total Alpha Acid Units Required $= 3·0 \times 4$ gals.

$$= 12·0 \text{ A.A.U.'s}$$

Goldings Hops to provide Total A.A.U.'s $\times \frac{2}{3} = 8$ A.A.U.'s

Progress Hops to provide $12 \times \frac{1}{3} = 4$ A.A.U.'s

Thus the amount of Golding Hops needed $= \dfrac{8}{4·0} = 2$ oz.

and Progress Hops needed $= \dfrac{4}{5·0} = 0·8$ oz.

Simple checks like these can be a worthwhile exercise for beginners and a useful back-up to experienced brewers, who normally make their selection based on hand appraisal.

Inadequate attention to hop rates, probably through ignorance, shows itself too frequently amongst home-brewed beer by incorrectly balanced bitterness. This state of affairs does not help at all in enhancing the reputation of home-brewing.

CHAPTER 11

Water

BEER is nearly all water! The commercial breweries' ability to demonstrate this fact has caused many a bar room argument over the years. Brewers have always shown a marked reluctance to associate their beers with water, and in the trade, brewing water is known as "liquor"; "water" is merely the liquid that is used for cleaning and washing plant and equipment.

The first insight into the theoretical side of brewing practice for new home-brewers is usually the adage that "soft waters are good for brewing dark beers and hard waters are good for brewing light beers". Although this statement is a gross oversimplification of the facts, it is basically true, and does serve as a useful guide in practice.

Old time brewers were quick to realise that certain water supplies were more suitable than others for brewing a particular type of beer. The major criteria in the selection of a site for these early breweries was the suitability of the water supply, and since it was rare to find a supply that was satisfactory for all types of beer, locations became famous for one particular beer. The Burton area was famous for its light beers, especially Pale Ales, Dublin for Stouts, and the London area for Dark Sweet Beers.

It was only when scientific knowledge advanced to an understanding of the chemical reactions of brewery processes that the effects of mineral salts were really appreciated. From this, full advantage can now be taken from a salt analysis to enable most water supplies to be adjusted to suit the brewing requirements for all types of beers.

Reasons for water treatment

Water treatment could be simply referred to as Acid Treatment. For instance, during the mashing process, the conversion of the malt starch to sugar can only take place if the mixture of the crushed grain and water is slightly acidic in nature.

So minute is the amount of acid needed that even the common salts found in ordinary water supplies are enough to upset the delicate reactions. Phosphates in the malt dissolve into the mashing water and react with the salts present to form a very dilute solution of acid phosphorus. The actual amount of acid formed is dependent on the types of malt used in the grist and the presence of certain sympathetic salts.

To understand this point, it is best to consider the theoretical case of Pale Malt grain mashed in distilled water (i.e. pure water) which is chemically neutral, i.e. neither acid nor alkaline. The amount of phosphates liberated into the distilled water under these conditions does not contribute enough acid to promote an efficient conversion from starch to sugar.

To bring the acid level up to the required value, either acid-forming salts or alternatively dark or roasted malts, which are inherently acidic, can be employed. Dark beers brewed from dark malts are usually self sufficient in acid and can therefore be brewed from low salt content water (soft water). Pale beers, on the other hand, can only resort to added hardening salts to preserve the colour and maintain acidity.

Many other factors can also influence the selection of water treatment. There are so many complex and sensitive reactions in the process of brewing that are influenced by the type of mineral salt present in the water, that it is impossible to satisfy all requirements.

The coagulation of protein matter, the production of yeast nutrients and flavour extraction from hops and malts, can all be altered by the addition or removal of certain salts.

Starting off with the right conditions for mashing invariably creates conditions acceptable for these other factors, so there is no real need to complicate the issue. Knowing a bit more about the basic ingredients, however, is always helpful in formulating recipes and sorting out snags if they occur.

Sources of brewing water

The main source of water used by home-brewers is from our household taps which are supplied with high quality, pure drinking water from the water authorities. Private wells, rain water and even distilled water can be utilised as brewing water so long as their individual characteristics can be assessed and any deficiencies rectified.

Most domestic water supplies originate from rain. The course of the water from rain to the tap involves many changes in its constituents. As the rain falls and drains through the soil it picks up minute quantities of mineral salts and organic matter. Depending on the natural geology of the landscape, the water either filters through porous rocks or strata to deep water wells, or it is channelled over the surface to form streams, rivers and lakes. Both courses result in a further modification to the salt content, thus it will be appreciated that, say, predominantly chalk areas will have a marked difference in its saline constituents from that of sand or clay strata.

Water authorities tap their supplies direct from the lakes, rivers and artificial reservoirs, or from bore holes to the deep water wells.

At the pumping station the water is filtered and purified of all harmful products before it is passed into the domestic service mains. Most of the original mineral salts remain in solution together with microscopic quantities of organic matter which pass through the fine filters. To maintain sterility and purity, small controlled doses of chlorine are added to the supply.

Very few domestic water supplies are entirely unsuitable for brewing purposes; many do, however, require some form of treatment to coax the best performances out of the brewing processes for quality beer production.

Acid and water treatment

The use of water treatment for acid adjustment would often seem an illogical approach to the problem to a wine-maker. In winemaking, any deficiency in the acid content of the starting ingredients can easily be rectified by the addition of small quantities of citric, malic or tartaric acids. As beer brewers, we are in a different situation regarding acidity. Acid is an essential part of fermentation, but its inclusion in wine is even more demanded for reasons of taste and flavour.

Acid tastes do not find favour in beer, so additions for that reason need never be used in beermaking. Also undesirable salts will be formed on reaction with the malt which adversely affect the flavour and the chemical reactions of mashing. In certain instances though, it may be thought pre-

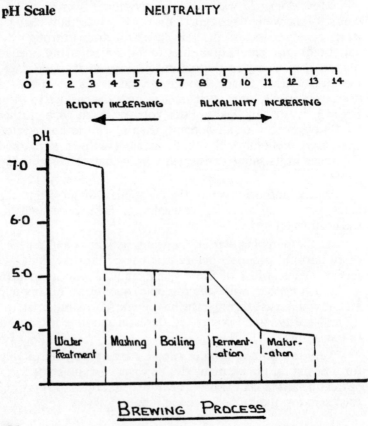

pH Scale   NEUTRALITY

ACIDITY INCREASING   ALKALINITY INCREASING

BREWING PROCESS

Changes in pH

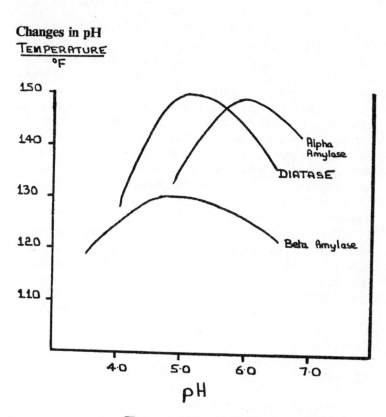

Temperature °F

150

140

130

120

110

Alpha Amylase

DIATASE

Beta Amylase

4·0   5·0   6·0   7·0

pH

ENZYME RESPONSE

ferable to use lactic acid to overcome problems not easily solved by other means.

pH and its implications

Similarly, the winemaker's method of determining acid and expressing it in terms of parts per thousand (p.p.t.) of sulphuric acid is quite inappropriate in beermaking. Brewing reactions are sensitive to the active acid present and not the quantity of acid as determined by titration.

Effective acidity is due to the hydrogen ion concentration and is represented in numbers on a logarithmic scale of pH. The scale runs from 1 to 14 with neutrality at 7. Values between 7 and 1 are acidic and 7 to 14 alkaline. Trying to grasp the fundamental concepts of pH for the purposes of practical reasoning can be a difficult task for the layman, including myself. For instance, I still have to think twice to assure myself that a *reduction* in the pH value means an *increase* in acidity, and I still cannot really comprehend that the difference between pH of 5·0 and 5·1 is about ten times greater than the difference between pH 6·0 and 6·1.

The problem lies in the fact that the pH value of a solution cannot be readily related to the titratable acidity. For instance, consider a gallon of wort with a titratable acidity of 10 parts per thousand that has a pH value of 4·0. By diluting the wort with another gallon of water, by definition the titratable acidity would be proportionally reduced to 5·0 parts per thousand. The pH value, though, might only change to 4·2: the actual figure being impossible to calculate.

This confusing aspect of pH is because changes in the value are the result of the *combined action of the acid and the other dissolved salts* that are in the solution. Ordinary mineral salts in our water supplies can promote or decrease the effective acidity.

Many brewing reactions require an increase in acidity. Certain dissolved solids can neutralise or "buffer" any attempt to alter the pH value by adding acid to the solution. Just as important, these substances can restrict the formation of vital acids formed within the barley malt.

The action of these substances is analogous to the buffers on a railway line. They absorb the "shock" of added acid. The ability to buffer is limited. Strong acids will overcome the absorbent effect of buffer substances to allow a reduction in pH value, just as a train driven at full steam will overcome the buffers at the end of the railway line!

Only weak organic acids are found in brewing ingredients and hence buffering considerations are extremely important. Neat acids are not normally used in brewing to alter pH; a reliance being mainly placed on mineral salts to make the subtle changes needed to create the optimum conditions for the reactions.

The behaviour of enzymes, proteins and other substances is dependent on the pH value of the environment in which the reactions takes place. There is a continual increase in the acidity from wort to beer (see fig: page 87). Measurement of the pH value at the various stages can be made as described in Chapter 16.

88

TABLE 1

Quantities in parts per million (or mgm/litre)

	soft	Moderately Hard	Very Hard
General chemical analysis			
Total Alkalinity as $CaCO_3$	24	265	240
Total Dissolved Solids (dried at 160°C)	51	370	1226
pH	7·4	7·95	7·2
Hardness			
Temporary Hardness as $CaCO_3$	24	260	235
Permanent Hardness as $CaCO_3$	9	35	622
Total Hardness as $CaCO_3$	33	295	857
Total Hardness as (°Clark)	2·3	21·0	60
Mineral analysis			
Calcium as Ca	11	114	268
Magnesium as Mg	—	3	62
Sodium as Na	24	13	30
Carbonate as $CaCO_3$	9	161	141
Chloride as Cl	—	17	36
Sulphate as SO_4	—	15	638
Nitrate as NO_3	—	12	31

WATER ANALYSIS

Using water analysis sheets

Draw off a pint of water from your kitchen tap. Hold it up to the light to check its clarity; swill it around the glass to release its bouquet, sample a small quantity to assess its flavour; and what do you have?—an almost tasteless, colourless, inert liquid, that defies all the human senses for accurate analysis.

One sample is virtually indistinguishable from another. Hydrometers, methylated spirits, iodine and other brewing test gear can give no clue whatsoever as to its chemical make-up. The mineral salts in water have an extremely important effect on brewing reactions, so it is essential that we know something about the subject.

Water treatment can be approached on a trial and error basis with moderate success. It is usually only when the domestic supply lends itself readily to water treatment that this approach is successful. In most cases, it leads to many disappointments in time and "hard cash" through sub-standard brews.

The best plan if embarking on a water treatment exercise is to obtain a copy of the water analysis of your domestic supply from your local Water Board. This highly technical data can then be used and interpreted in terms and quantities more familiar to the average home-brewer.

So that comparisons can be made with the utmost relevance, I have listed in Table 1 , the analyses for three typical domestic supplies ranging from very soft to very hard waters. The list is by no means complete, for I have omitted some of the "deadwood data" to avoid confusion.

Hardness of water

Water is broadly classified by its degree of Hardness. Most people, especially housewives and home-brewers, can assess with a fair degree of accuracy whether their supply is hard or soft. The layman's assessment is based on taste and by observing certain physical properties. For instance, hard waters precipitate salts on boiling—the "fur" in kettles—and soft waters readily promote a lather from soap solutions I gather that even water chemists used to determine hardness years ago by testing the foam forming properties of samples of water with standard soap solutions. Nowadays, hardness is determined more scientifically.

Hardness relates to the amount of Calcium and Magnesium Salts that are in solution. The combined quantity of bicarbonates, carbonates and sulphates of these two salts is referred to as TOTAL HARDNESS.

Units of hardness are Clark's degrees, which are directly proportional to the amount of hard salts in solution as is shown in Table 2, i.e. Clarks degress = p.p.m. $\times 0.07$

TABLE 2		
Classification	Total Hardness p. p. m. mgm/litre	Clarks Degrees
Soft	0–100	0–7
Medium soft	100–200	7–14
Moderately hard	200–400	14–28
Hard	400–600	28–42
Very hard	Above 600	Above 42

If the bicarbonates of Magnesium and Calcium are present in water, their solubility is not stable. On boiling, carbon dioxide gas is driven off, reverting the bicarbonate salt to the insoluble carbonate state, which will precipitate out of solution on cooling. Since they are no longer soluble, by definition they cannot contribute to PERMANENT HARDNESS. The removal of these salts brings about a reduction in the hardness of the water and thus it is signified as TEMPORARY HARDNESS. Sulphates of Magnesium and Calcium are unaffected by boiling and remain in solution as permanent hardness.

The information regarding hardness is the most important data on the analysis sheet as far as we as brewers are concerned.

Temporary and permanent hardness have a directly opposite effect on the brewing reactions.

Most types of beer require some form of hardness in the water. The old saying that "soft waters for dark beers and hard waters for light beers" would be better modified as **"Temporarily hard waters are good for dark beers and Permanently hard waters are good for light beers"**. It is only really special cases, for instance Pale Lager, that can be brewed using untreated soft water.

The first consideration in brewing must always be to create the best environment for the enzymes to work in the mashing stage. Salts of temporary hardness cause alkalinity and those of permanent hardness promote acidity. Since brewing reactions need, and are critically sensitive to, the amount of acidity in the mash liquor, then obviously the *quantity* and the *type* of hardness that is present is extremely important.

The maximum tolerable quantity of carbonates in brewing water is about 150 p.p.m. To be able to maintain the correct acidity with this concentration of alkalinity would probably call for the inclusion of about 20 per cent of dark roasted malts in the formulation of the grist. The strong flavouring properties of the malts prohibit the use of greater quantities than this and thus set the top limit on the amount of carbonates than can be present in the mashing stage.

Carbonates, which constitute the major proportion of temporary hardness, are not completely insoluble and most waters, even after boiling, can still support about 30–40 p.p.m. of these salts. At this level, they are relatively harmless and can for most practical purposes be ignored.

The figures for the moderately hard water show quite well the solubility of the carbonates. In this water there is very little contribution of sulphates to the total hardness thus practically all hardness is of a temporary nature.

By boiling, 260 p.p.m. of temporary hardness can be removed to leave just 35 p.p.m. in solution as permanent hardness. This action can therefore render the "moderately hard" water "very soft" (see Table 2)

The "very hard" water on the other hand will leave 857–235 p.p.m.=622 p.p.m. of hardness after boiling, which, although it is much softer, will still be classified as very hard, This is due to the fact that this water is very rich in calcium sulphate. Even with this level of permanent hardness, it would still be advisable to boil off most of the alkalinity before using it for Light Beer production.

The pH value will indicate whether the water is acid or alkaline. Figures above 7·0 show that the water is alkaline and below 7·0 that it is acidic. Moderately hard water has a pH of 7·95 due to the high proportion of temporary hardness. An estimated figure of 7·2 has been given for the very hard water which is based on the fact that sulphates alone do not have much effect on the pH of water. It is only in reaction with malt phosphates that the effect is noticed.

The figures for the Total Dissolved Solids include all the salts that form hardness, plus the "soft" salts such as Chlorides, Nitrates, etc., and also any organic matter that may be in solution.

Probably the most confusing aspect of the Water Analysis Sheet to most of us is that there is rarely any reference to the physical quantities of the common salts that are in solution.

The document does not list the amounts of Calcium Sulphate (Gypsum), Calcium Carbonate (Chalk) and Magnesium Sulphate (Epsom Salts) that are present. Most home-brewers would naturally consider this data as being an essential starting point for any water treatment exercise.

Water Board chemists find it much easier and much more useful, for their purposes, to analyse the water into its constituent metal and salt compounds. For instance, the "Calcium as Ca" figure embraces all the calcium derived from Calcium Sulphate and Calcium Carbonate. From our point of view this is most irritating since for this particular case, Calcium Sulphate is an acid salt, and Calcium Carbonate is an alkaline salt, and thus have completely opposite effects on the brewing reactions.

By delving into the chemistry a bit further, it is possible to calculate the tendency of the salts to increase or decrease the mash acidity. To make life easier, the assumption that all the alkalinity is due to calcium carbonate, and all acid promotion is due to Calcium Sulphate is quite adequate.

TABLE 3

Add 1 teaspoonful (5 ml) in 5 gallons of water of:—	Will add the following p.p.m. to the Water Analysis figures							
	Ca	Mg	Na	K	CO₃	SO₄	Cl	Total
Calcium Sulphate (Gypsum)	50	—	—	—	—	125	—	175
Magnesium Sulphate (Epsom Salts)	—	15	—	—	—	60	—	75
Sodium Chloride (Common Salt)	—	—	125	—	—	—	200	325
Calcium Carbonate (Precipitated Chalk)	30	—	—	—	50	—	—	80
Potassium Chloride	—	—	—	200	—	—	150	350

Even the Water Board chemists make a similar assumption. All data is expressed in terms that can be identified as elements or salt compounds. For example, the "temporary hardness as $CaCO_3$" does not mean that this hardness is entirely due to Calcium Carbonate ($CaCO_3$). What it really means is that the combined effect of all the salts of temporary hardness (i.e. Calcium and Magnesium Carbonates) have the *equivalent chemical effect* of the stated quantity of $CaCO_3$.

The only way that we can make use of this analysis sheet, then, is to convert the common salts that we use for water treatment into similar terms. I have calculated the approximate chemical contribution of adding 1 level teaspoonful (5 ml.) of these salts to five gallons of water. The quantities are based on average figures taken by spooning the salts out of their containers, and levelling off the surplus from the rim of the teaspoon with the back of a knife blade. Although I have made some broad assumptions, the following table is accurate enough for our purposes.

The following example demonstrates the use of the above table to modify the saline constituents for the moderately hard water by a treatment applied in three stages:—

1. Add 2 teaspoonsful of Gypsum
2. Add 1 teaspoonful of Epsom Salts
3. Boil to remove the Temporary Hardness.

For this latter exercise, it is assumed that all the 260 p.p.m. of temporary hardness has been removed, and in the ratio of 30 : 50 between Ca and CO_3 (i.e. Ca=100 CO_3=160).

The water before treatment would be classed as a Carbonate liquor and not really suited for mashing without some form of modification. By adding hardening salts and boiling, the Sulphate content has increased dramatically and the Carbonate content almost eliminated to make the water ideally suited for brewing Pale Ales. By omitting the Gypsum and Epsom Salts, and restricting the boiling time, an excellent Stout liquor could be produced.

Mineral salt requirements

The next stage in the water treatment exercise is to find out the types and quantities of salts that need to be pre-

TABLE 4

Before Treatment		Water Treatment			
Part of the original Analysis for the Moderately Hard Water		Stage 1 Add 2 tpfl. Gypsum $Ca+SO_4$ $(100+250)=350$	Stage 2 Add 1 tpfl. Epsom Salts $Mg+SO_4$ $(15+60)=75$	Stage 3 Boil/remove Precipitated Chalk $Ca+CO_3$ $(100+160)=260$	After treatment
Total Alkalinity as $CaCO_3$	265	$=265$	$=265$	$-260=5$	5
Total Dissolved Solids	370	$+350=720$	$+75=795$	$-260=535$	535
Temporary Hardness as $CaCO_3$	260	$=260$	$=260$	$-260=0$	0
Permanent Hardness as $CaCO_3$	35	$+350=385$	$+75=460$	$=460$	460
Total Hardness as $CaCO_3$	295	$+350=645$	$+75=720$	$-260=460$	460
Calcium as Ca	114	$+100=214$	$=214$	$-100=114$	114
Magnesium as Mg	3	$=3$	$+15=18$	$=18$	18
Carbonate as CO_3	161	$=161$	$=161$	$-160=1$	1
Sulphate as SO_4	15	$+250=265$	$+60=325$	$=325$	325
Sodium as Na	13	Unchanged by Treatment			13
Chloride as Cl	1	Unchanged by Treatment			17
Nitrates as NO_3	127	Unchanged by Treatment			12

96

sent for brewing the various types of beer, and how these salts affect the brewing reactions.

Luckily for us, research in the commercial field has led to a general agreement as to the particular salts that are needed to complement our brewing ingredients. The table below shows the concentration levels of the salts that have a major influence on the character of the beer. Recommended maximum and minimum levels quoted allow for the differences in formulation of the grist, and other factors, such as flavour and the presence of other minor salts which can reflect back in some way on the finished beer.

The table is very limited in its content, in that only a small selection of beers and mineral salts have been evaluated. It must be appreciated that the object was not to give a complete analysis to cover all cases, but merely to present a broad picture of the exercise in hand. The beers have been chosen to emphasise the vast difference in salt requirements.

In the upper Common Salt section, the quantities are expressed in terms of parts per million (p.p.m.). Now that we are in the Common Market, you may find some data being expressed in milligrams per litre (mgm/l) which is just the metric equivalent of our English system. The quantities have the same value, i.e. 1 p.p.m. = 1 mgm/1., so there should be no confusion over this point if the occasion arises. Both systems have been devised to express the small quantities as realistic and manageable units.

One lb. (16 oz.) of a salt made up to one gallon (160 fluid ounces) is known as a 10 per cent solution. Alternatively it can be described as containing 100,000 parts per million of the salt.

Considering that typical water supplies only contain up to about 500 p.p.m., we are working in very minute quantities indeed. In more familiar terms, the average water supply contains only about half a teaspoonful of solids in every gallon. This really brings it into perspective and indicates the overpowering effect of just adding another teaspoonful of salt to your brewing water.

The latter section of the table is just the chemical breakdown of the recommended salts as given in the Common Salt section. It is essential that this reconstruction of the data has been carried out so that it will be compatible with the

TABLE 5

COMMON SALT	PALE ALES p.p.m.	MILD ALES p.p.m.	STOUTS p.p.m.	1 tpfl. in 5 gal is equal to:
Calcium Sulphate	350–550	70–200	—	175 p.p.m.
Magnesium Sulphate	60–120	40–60	60	75 "
Sodium Chloride	30–60	60–120	120–180	325 "
Potassium Chloride	—	60–120	120–180	350 "
Calcium Carbonate	30	30	100–150	80 "
Mineral analysis				Use in conjunction with Water Analysis
Ca	100–175	30–60	40–60	
Mg	12–25	8–12	12	
Na	10–20	20–40	40–60	
K	—	30–60	60–90	
Cl	15–25	50–100	100–150	
CO_3	15	15	50–75	
SO_4	300–500	80–200	—	

presentation of the mineral salt content as listed on the Water Analysis Sheet. By comparing the two lists it is possible to calculate the quantities and types of salts that are needed to modify your brewing water to suit the particular beer that you intend to brew.

Examples of these calculations were given in the previous section. All measurements were calculated in terms of level teaspoonsful (5 ml.). Adjustments should only be attempted to an accuracy of the nearest ¼ teaspoonful. Trying to adjust to the nearest p.p.m. is virtually impossible, and is indeed impracticable and unnecessary.

The main group of salts that concern us are the sulphates, carbonates and chlorides, and it is interesting to discuss why these particular salts are recommended for certain beers and not for others.

Sulphates

Calcium Sulphate, commonly known as Gypsum or Plaster of Paris, is an extremely useful salt for water treatment. It occurs naturally in many water supplies where its solubility contributes to permanent hardness. The Burton area, which is abundantly rich in this salt, is renowned for the quality of its brewing water.

Water is capable of supporting very large concentrations of calcium sulphate without incurring any harmful side effects to the beer. The main attribute of Gypsum is its ability to react with phosphates in the malt during mashing to form beneficial acids. Efficient mash reactions, good breaks, and the coagulation of protein matter, with resultant clarity in the final beer can be secured in Pale Ales brewed from water containing large quantities of this salt. Gypseous water also permits the use of higher hop rates, and the inclusion of the more strongly flavoured, high alpha acid content hops in the formulation.

Magnesium Sulphate is the other salt which partners Calcium Sulphate in forming permanent hardness. The performance of this salt is just as beneficial as Gypsum, with the added bonus that it contributes to the yeast nutrient properties of the wort. Regrettably, it has an unpleasant bitter flavour that mars its usefulness if present in too large a proportion. I like to exclude this salt from all brews based on more than one pound of malt per gallon. For lighter gravity brews I replace about a third of the Gypsum with Magnesium Sulphate to ensure adequate yeast nutrients.

The common source of Magnesium Sulphate is as Epsom Salts, and I am sure that most people are aware of the side effects of taking too large a dose of salts!

Sodium Sulphate is not very often present in water as a predominant salt. Small quantities are acceptable but it becomes increasingly embarrassing as the intensity rises. The sodium salt is noted for its characteristic hard and harsh flavour which is very difficult to eliminate or mask.

Sulphates in general impart a drier flavour to the beer and a certain cleanness to the palate. Light Ales, Bitters and even Mild Ales are grateful for a bit of sulphate hardness in their brewing water. As a rough guide, the need for hardening salts decreases as the proportion of dark roasted acidic malts increases. Pale Ales demand the maximum, reducing through Light Ales, Bitters, Milds, Brown Ales, to its omission for the darkest Stouts.

Pale Lagers, however, are a case on their own, as they do not like too many sulphates, especially the Magnesium and Sodium salts.

Chlorides

Sodium Chloride, common household salt, is the only Chloride found naturally in appreciable quantities in our water. Chloride has always been held as an essential constituent for fullness in dark ales, with the notable exception of Stouts of the Dublin type. The certain roundness on the palate given by com..1on salt is accompanied by increased hop bitterness, and makes this salt eminently suited for all types of sweet beers. Being readily available, it tends to become a popular salt for Chloride adjustment. Unfortunately, high concentrations have a harmful effect on yeast activity, and levels should preferably be kept within the range quoted in Table 5.

Calcium and Potassium Chlorides are preferred commercially for salt adjustments. These Chlorides behave in a similar fashion to Gypsum in increasing mash acidity as well as increasing the Chloride content of the water. Calcium Chloride, although a versatile salt, however, is not an easy salt for the amateur to dispense accurately and consequently the alternative, Potassium Chloride, is to be preferred. All chloride adjustments should ideally consist mainly of Potassium Chloride together with a smaller contribution of common salt.

Carbonates

Requirements for carbonate water vary considerably. Dark beers, especially those containing a high proportion of roasted malts, like some alkalinity derived from the carbonates to balance the extra acidity in the grist. Pale Lagers and all light coloured beers on the other hand, can be ruined by carbonate hardness. The effect is to reduce the acidity away from the optimum for efficient mash reactions to take place. The carbonates of Calcium and Magnesium are insoluble and are mainly formed as a result of the boiling action on their respective bicarbonate salts. Waters containing these two salts can be used for Pale Ale production by racking the clear soft water from the insoluble precipitate, and adding a requisite amount of sulphates.

Sodium Carbonate presents more of a problem since it is highly soluble and cannot be removed by boiling. Some waters with appreciable amounts of this salt, especially in the London area, must be restricted to the production of the sweeter dark beers, since it is virtually impossible to reduce this alkalinity without adversely affecting other desirable characteristics of the water.

The other important factor of carbonate waters is the effect on hop flavour. Hop bitterness becomes increasingly more harsh and clinging with higher concentrations of these salts. Where a delicate hop flavour is not needed, as in the case of heavier bodied dark beers, carbonate waters may be regarded as hop savers. The flavour would be unpalatable and overpowering if used with generously hopped light coloured beers.

Nitrates

Nitrates are usually only found in minor quantities in brewing water. Even in trace quantities their presence can have a marked effect on the health of yeast. The effect is only noticeable after a day or so of fermentation when the attenuation of wort and the reproduction of the yeast is noticeably slowed down. Pitching a fresh yeast for every brew is the best method of minimising this trouble. Levels should preferably be kept below 30 p.p.m.

Water treatment

As amateurs, we must be prepared in some cases to compromise in our efforts to emulate to correct brewing liquor for all beers. Ion exchange units and water softening plant as used by commerical breweries are just not stocked by home-brew shops!

In some areas, the water supply is only suited to making certain beers and efforts to render it acceptable for all types can be tedious and time consuming. These cases are rare, but where a particular area is say, only really good for light coloured beers, it quite often follows that the beer loving fraternity in the district uphold the local tradition and only favour drinking these ales. To satisfy everyone's needs, though, I have included adjustments to cover all classes of waters for all the common types of beers. The summary table for water treatment below should only be treated as a guide and not be rigidly adhered to. Local conditions and above all, where flavour is involved, personal preferences must be taken into account.

Water treatment falls into three main categories.

1. Addition of beneficial salts
2. Removal of unwanted salts
3. Dilution of harmful salts.

Five salts, Calcium Sulphate (Gypsum), Magnesium Sulphate (as Epsom Salts), Sodium Chloride (Common Salt), Calcium Carbonate (as Precipitate of Chalk) and Potassium Chloride, which comprise our beneficial salts must be pure compounds and preferably of B.P. Pharmaceutical standard. For simplicity, the additions are given in level teaspoonsfu (5 ml.) of the dry substances.

The treatment is listed numerically on the table and the detailed instructions given below. Certain waters require several separate treatments. Each task must be implemented in

SUMMARY OF WATER TREATMENT

Type	Water authority analysis		Barley Wine	Pale Ale	Lager	Light Ale	Bitter	Mild	Brown Ale	Sweet Stout	Dry Stout
	Characteristics	Total solids									
Soft	Mixed salts in various proportions	Below 100	3:5	4:5	1	3:5	3:6	3:6	8:6:9	8:6:9	7
Medium soft	Contains small quantity of temporary hardness	100–200	3:5:11	4:5:11	11	3:5:11	4:6:11	3:6	6:9	6:9	8
Moderately hard	Mostly temporary hardness	200–400	3:5:2	2:5:2	2	3:5:2	2	2:6	6:9:11	6:9:11	11
Hard	Temporary and permanent hardness	400–600	2	2	2	3:2	2:6	2	2:10:6	11:10:6	11
Very hard	Mainly permanent hardness	Above 600	2	2	2	2	2:6	2:10:6	2:10	11:10	11:10

the sequence given in the table. For example, when treating a hard water for Light Ale, the addition of one teaspoonful of Gypsum (3) must be added to every 5 gallons of "hard" water before boiling for half an hour (2). The reason is, in this instance, is that the presence of Gypsum in the boiling water assists in the removal of the ˙nwanted carbonates.

Problem waters, for example those containing high concentrations of the bicarbonates, chlorides or sulphates of Sodium, nitrates, or very hard Gypseous liquors, can only be brought down to manageable levels by dilution.

Rainwater, being devoid of any appreciable quantities of salts, is a convenient means of weakening the saline constituents of these liquors. Collection is only advisable in areas free from atmospheric pollution and also where the method of collection is free from contamination (e.g. roofs, gutters, pipes, etc.). It is essential that the rainwater is filtered and boiled thoroughly before use to ensure that it is absolutely pure and sterile.

Distilled water, if you are fortunate enough to find a cheap source of known purity, is even better as a diluent. Be wary of supplies from friends in the garage trade, as some "distilled" waters contain additives for use in electric batteries.

Remember that when diluting harmful salts with rain or distilled water, all the salts present in the original water are diluted to the same degree. Beneficial salts may need supplementing after this treatment.

The overriding factor in the treatments listed below must be to ensure that the acidity of the mash is satisfactory. The object of the exercise is to create a mash acidity of around a pH of 5.2. It may be necessary with some waters to increase the acidity by adding more sulphates, or conversely to decrease acidity by adding more carbonates, than the recommended doses given in the summary chart.

Treatment
1. No treatment required.
2. Boil all the water for half an hour. Allow to cool, and rack off the softer water from the chalk precipitate.
3. Add 1 level teaspoonful of Gypsum.
4. Add 2 level teaspoonsful of Gypsum.
5. Add ½ level teaspoonful of Epsom Salts.

6. Add ½ level teaspoonful of Potassium Chloride.
7. Add 1 level teaspoonful of Precipitate of Chalk.
8. Add ½ level teaspoonful of Precipitate of Chalk.
9. Add ½ level teaspoonful of Common Salt.
10. Dilute with Rainwater/Distilled water to bring the total dissolved solids down to a lower hardness category.
11. Bring all the water to the boil and allow to cool before racking.

CHAPTER 12

Yeast

YEAST is one of the lowest forms of plant life and has the ability to rapidly multiply in sugar solutions, leaving in its wake the sugar split roughly into equal quantities of alcohol and carbon dioxide gas.

Reproduction is by budding and fission, the daughter cells breaking away from the parent and starting the chain again. Such is the vigour of yeast life, that sometimes the daughter cells will mature before detachment, and actually form clusters running into several generations.

There are many types of yeast, each one peculiar to the environment and the saccharine matter on which it lives. The performance is such that each yeast is very sensitive to changes, and will generally only be suited to working in the conditions of its birth.

Thus the fermentation of beer should be confined to those yeasts that are sympathetic to the conditions in wort. Brewers Yeast (Saccharomyces Cerevisiae) is the particular strain used in this country for our top fermenting ales. Never use Bakers Yeast or Wine Yeasts (except for Barley Wine) in home-brewing. Actually, the term "top fermenting" is really classifying the characteristic of this yeast and describes the buoyancy and ability of the yeast crop to remain on the surface of the beer after the primary fermentation.

Bottom fermenters (Saccharomyces Carlsbergenis, or lager yeasts) are pure strains in which the yeast crop sinks in the wort after the primary fermentation.

The following sources of yeast are available to the amateur:—

1. Dried granules or tablets
2. Cultures
3. Commercial Beers.

The dried granules or tablets are the most convenient and most popular source of yeast for home-brewing. A teaspoonful, tablet, or small sachet of these yeasts is capable of producing a satisfactory fermentation for the average sized home-brew.

Theoretically, just one yeast cell would do the trick. By the natural processes of reproduction and multiplication by doubling every generation, enough yeast could be produced to turn all the sugar to alcohol and CO_2 gas. This is perfectly true, but in practice it would not prove to be a very satisfactory arrangement. Wort is a very vulnerable liquid and relies heavily on the Brewers yeast and fermentation process to provide a barrier against infection from other micro-organisms. The physical barrier and the blanket of CO_2 gas provided by a vigorously working yeast crop normally afford this protection.

The first criterion of a successful fermentation, then, is the speed at which the yeast can provide a barrier to infection. Unprotected worts should not be left more than eight hours without some sign of surface activity.

The safest way over the problem is to activate the yeast sometime before it is actually needed in the main brew.

Starter bottle

A yeast starter should be used for every brew. The pitching of a vigorously working yeast ensures that the fermentation will be off to a good start and can instil in the brewer great comfort and confidence for the subsequent success of the brew.

The starter is made up by cultivating a small quantity of yeast in a mixture of malt and sugar within the confines of a small loosely capped sterilised bottle. The time it takes to reach pitching condition is mainly dependent on the amount of yeast with which the bottle is started. A spoonful of dried yeast or a tablet will be ready within a matter of hours.

Yeast cultures and strains raised from commercial beers can, on the other hand, take days before activity is visible. Commercial brewery yeasts are generally far superior to the dried granular varieties that you can buy; some of which, I am sure, are of doubtful origin.

Commercial yeasts

Guinness is the only readily available naturally conditioned bottled beer. "Naturally conditioned" means that the gas conditioning in the bottle is derived from yeast. Guinness yeast is the best yeast I have come across for brewing top fermenting beers. The excellent properties of this strain can easily be ruined. Yeast is very susceptible to changes in its gravity and nutrient properties of the wort, and to perpetuate its hereditary attributes, it must be cultivated in a like environment; in this case, an all malt wort with a gravity of between SG of 40-50. Reproduction in, say, a plain sugar syrup would ruin the strain within a few generations. The cell shape would elongate to give a larger surface area to absorb more nutrient food.

Another source of good yeast is from the ordinary draught beers (not keg) in the pubs. So long as you don't go in the pub with your sample jar looking like the Weights and Measures Inspector, most barmen will let you take away a pint of draught. The procedure is to leave the beer in a sterile bottle overnight to allow for some precipitation of yeast, and then pour off gently the top three quarters of a pint (and drink!) and make up the starter with the remainder.

One of the best yeasts from draught is the Whitbread "B" Strain, a popular variety now used by many breweries. Although it is a first class yeast it has a low cycle rate, meaning that a fresh yeast culture needs to be cultivated after every sixth or seventh pitching. Taking a sample from the pub has the disadvantage that we do not really know how far the yeast has gone in its generation cycle, so when using the "B" strain it is better for us to make up a fresh starter for each brew and not rely on repitching with yeast from the previous brew.

108

I have also heard good reports of a lager yeast obtained from draught Skol, which sounded very interesting indeed, and will certainly be one that I will try in the near future.

Yeast cultures

Cultures of most commercial strains can be obtained for a small fee from laboratories that specialise in yeast cultivation.* The yeast is supplied on a gelatine slant in a test tube. Growing time is much longer and more tedious than other methods, which, except for specialised brews, makes this system less favourable on the grounds of effort.

Saving yeast

Yeast can be saved from one brew to start the next one. I personally have mixed feelings about the idea. The principles are basically sound and it's the implementation of them that causes the problems. Commercial breweries in this country have always used this system, and some have been able to keep the same strain of yeast going for over 30 years. The advantages are consistency of flavour and economy.

In home-brewing we do not have the resources of the laboratory equipment needed for selecting and checking healthy cells of the yeast, so consequently our interpretation is a rather hit or miss affair.

"Wet" yeast is very difficult to keep, and generally must be used again within one week of its original pitching. Any home-brewer who has been lucky enough to build up to a continuous fermentation situation where he is pitching one wort directly after racking another, can use this system with real advantage. Yeast crops multiply about ten times their weight in the period of primary fermentation, and thus only a fraction of this is needed to start the next brew. The rest can be discarded.

Only the yeast from brews over an original gravity of 40 are suitable for re-pitching. The yeasts reproduced by light gravity beers are seldom suitable.

Yeast for re-pitching must be selected with great care. The first and final crop should not be used since the former

*The Brewing Industry Research Centre, Nutfield, Surrey.

contains hop residues and the latter a high proportion of dead cells.

Select a sample from the middle crop beneath the skin of the pancake head. "Pat" off the protective coat with the back of a wooden spoon to reveal the light, clean looking yeast underneath. These surface cells should be fairly well drained and free of beer. Scrape off a few teaspoonsful on to a piece of absorbent paper and leave for a few minutes to drain. Mould the yeast into a ball and wrap in a small square of clear polythene and secure with an elastic band. Put the sample into a small jar and store in the freezer compartment of your refrigerator.

The ball freezes rock hard but will keep far better than most other methods.

When the yeast is required, a starter is made up in the usual way.

Always inspect yeast before making up the starter. Healthy yeast should show no signs of sloppiness nor an unpleasant "rusty" colour. By getting into the habit of tasting a small sample of the yeast before using it, experience will soon be gained in detecting those that have gone off. In really bad cases, the yeast will give off a disagreeable odour.

CHAPTER 13

Cleaning

THE best advice I can give on cleaning equipment is to train someone else to do it for you. Ultimately, keeping equipment and utensils clean and hygienic saves time, money and your temper. Cleaning is an unenviable task and there is a temptation for beginners to the craft to disregard the advice and omit these practices. I know I did, and it was not until I had to pour a five gallon brew down the drain through infection, that I really started to take notice and implement the advice I had been given on cleaning and sterilising. Infection multiplies with astonishing rapidity.

It is worthwhile considering the cleaning aspect when choosing your armoury for the brewhouse. Any time that can be saved on this chore by selecting equipment that is easy to keep clean will always be gratefully appreciated at a later date by your "bottle washer"; especially if it is yourself! With the exception of the boiler, all the other equipment needed for the brewery can be made of plastic or glass.

Beer is very sensitive to ordinary household detergents and cleaning powders. The minutest traces of detergents and grease can destroy the head of beer. The taste is usually unaffected, but a headless beer looks incomplete and unattractive and for these reasons, washing up liquids should be avoided where possible.

Hot water and a good scrubbing brush will make short work of cleaning the larger items, such as dustbins, buckets and boilers. Stubborn deposits can be removed with one of these nylon wool scouring pads. Nylon pads are far better than the wire wool type and are virtually everlasting; they can even be sterilised by boiling water. Until I started to use these pads, one of the worse deposits to remove was the ring of yeast and hop resins which accumulate at the surface level of the fermentation in the dustbin. Always clean vessels immediately after use before the deposit hardens and trouble sets in. The larger vessels are much easier and accessible to clean than the small articles. I have not yet been able to find a simple way of cleaning an air lock!

The natural standards of cleanliness that are applied to the utensils used in the home for the preparation of food and drink should be maintained for the brewing and serving of beer. Consider beermaking as an extension of cooking and implement the same rigid standards of hygiene that you would naturally apply to the task.

Brewing has the same disadvantage as preparing a meal; the washing-up afterwards.

STERILISATION

Reasons for sterilisation

Beer is probably the most delicate of all alcoholic drinks and is very susceptible to infection at all stages of its production. The sugary malt liquid is an ideal breeding ground for all sorts of airborne bacteria which can render a brew worthless in a very short space of time.

The standard procedures of brewing usually quite adequately prevent infection of the beer. Most of the harmful bacteria are either killed or inhibited in their action by solutions of alcohol. The higher the alcohol the better is the protection afforded against infection. In fact, spirits such as Whisky and Brandy, have been used to sterilise flesh wounds in cases of emergency. No doubt that you have noticed this with regular monotony in the T.V. Westerns!

The alcohol content of finished beer rarely exceeds 7 per cent and thus does not in itself provide much protection against infection. It is interesting to note that hops were initially added to beer only to improve its keeping qualities, although now they are included solely for reasons of taste.

Beer also contains very little acid; the other natural preservative. Wine, the next type of drink up on the alcoholic scale, relies quite heavily on the acid content to keep it sound. An acid taste is not desirable in beer since it leads to a "cidery" flavour.

Not being well endowed with natural preservatives beer, it can be appreciated, relies largely on the care taken by the brewer in preventing contamination. "Prevention" is the key word in brewing, for an infected brew is difficult, and in most cases impossible, to rectify afterwards.

In the brewing process, the wort, or beer, passes through a number of different containers, and in doing so it also comes into contact with various utensils, such as thermometers, spoons and syphon tubes, etc. There is obviously a risk that any one of these items could transfer infection and off flavours to the others and subsequently to the finished beer.

Thorough cleansing and sterilisation of all items immediately before use is obviously very important.

Sterilising agents

The two types of sterilising agents commonly used for home brewing are either Chlorine based or Sulphur Dioxide based. Both types can be made up to any strength.

Chlorine is by far the best sterilising agent, but unfortunately, it can be dangerous if it is not used and handled sensibly. This is why I usually prefer to use Sulphur Dioxide based agents where possible, and just leave the Chlorine type for heavily contaminated articles.

Bleach

The most convenient source of chlorine for sterilising can be obtained from using ordinary household bleach, e.g. Domestos. Made up to 10 per cent strength by topping up two fluid ounces of neat bleach to one pint of water, it makes a really effective sterilising agent. Chlorine at this strength will kill any wild yeast and bacteria. Heavily contaminated equipment should be washed with this 10 per cent

113

solution and allowed to stand "wet" for a few minutes. After this short soaking, the equipment should be thoroughly rinsed to remove all detectable traces of the chlorine. Chlorine has that distinctive "swimming bath" smell.

Sulphur Dioxide, the other type of sterilising agent, is incompatible with chlorine. When the two are mixed together they effectively cancel each other out. This phenomenon is extremely useful as it means that any traces of chlorine left on the equipment can be chemically neutralised by washing the item again with a 10 per cent solution of Sodium Metabisulphite before finally rinsing the item with water.

The bleach treatment should only be necessary on ill treated articles such as bottles and gallon jars that one acquires secondhand in a dirty state. Another case needing this treatment would be if your brews and equipment had been contaminated with a "bug" which did not respond to normal sterilising practices. Always use chlorine based sterilisers in a well-ventilated room.

Sodium metabisulphite

Commonly abbreviated to "Sodium Met" by home-brewers, the chemical is a convenient source of sulphur dioxide and is the most versatile of all sterilising agents available for brewing. It can be regarded as a yeast inhibitor and not a yeast killer like chlorine. By varying the strength of the solution to suit, it can be used for sterilising equipment and also be added to the finished beer as a preservative. In fact, it is the only preservative allowed by law in commercial beer.

Again, the most convenient strength is a 10 per cent solution, which is made up by dissolving 2 ounces of the white powder in hot water to give a total volume of one pint.

Two ounces of this solution diluted down with a pint of hot water provides a normal stock mix for general sterilisation of bottles, jars, dustbins and instruments. The solution can be taken as being effective so long as the pungent sulphur dioxide smell can be detected. If there is any doubt over this point, add a pinch of citric acid to the solution which should result in a spontaneous release of the obnoxious gas. Always make up a fresh stock solution for each sterilising session and discard afterwards. The articles should just be washed or filled with this solution and left "wet" for a few minutes before rinsing thoroughly with cold water.

Milton

Milton is a commercially prepared sterilising agent marketed for general home use. It is a very efficient product and can be used with confidence in our breweries, but it is rather expensive, and is no more effective than our home prepared solutions.

Silana P.F.

Heavily contaminated vessels and containers where the shape prohibits the use of direct mechanical cleaning, can be treated with Silana P.F. Crystals. The compound, when made up to recommended dose as a hot solution, will remove the most stubborn stains and deposits from your brewing gear. Ideal for cleaning polythene cubes, dustbins, gallon jars and even wooden barrels.

Seeing in the dark!

Beer bottles are usually a dark brown or green colour. One of the original reasons for dark coloured bottles was to hide the yeast deposit precipitated by the secondary fermentation in the bottles. It is all very well, but it is very difficult to check that the insides are clean before bottling.

The best method of checking to see if a dark coloured glass container is dirty, is to fill it with water and hold it up towards a strong light. Even minute deposits on the sides are clearly shown up by the illuminating and magnifying power of the water inside the bottle.

I must have wasted hours of valuable brewing time on this chore before I discovered this simple dodge.

Squeezy bottle steriliser

One of the most useful aids in my brewery is my Squeezy bottle steriliser dispenser. It is actually just an empty washing-up liquid bottle that has been thoroughly cleansed of its original contents and filled with sterilising solution. It can hold a pint of the standard stock solution. By squeezing a small amount in each empty bottle or jar before storage these containers can be kept sweet until they are ready for use again. The cap of the dispenser bottle must always be replaced after use to prevent the sulphur dioxide gas evaporating and the solution losing its strength.

Stock solutions in this dispenser eliminate the tedious procedure of having to make up small quantities of solution everytime you want to sterilise a few articles.

Clearly label the bottle and keep well out of the way of the searching hands of children.

Bottle brush

Gallon jars, bottles, plastic cubes and barrels have narrow necks, so cleaning calls for a bottle brush to give access to the inside surfaces.

The common type of brush just consists of nylon bristles trapped radially between a wire twist and shaped to form a cylindrical shape slightly larger than the inside dia-diameter of the bottle. The wire handle can be bent and formed to suit larger bottles and jars if required. I have found that these brushes are inadequate for many jobs. The hard tip does most of the work by mechanically pushing off the deposits. The bristles usually only just score lines on the yeast film that forms on the inside of containers which have held beer. These surfaces really need to be wiped, and not scraped. The biggest drawback is that considerable force is needed to push the bristly head of the brush through the narrow neck. It is a physically exhausting task to clean any number of bottles using this device, so I had a go at designing my own. The result was so successful, that I am prepared to divulge the details of my crude handiwork. This simple aid has cut bottle washing time by 80 per cent and has literally saved me hours of toil and hardwork.

The materials required are:—

 1 Foam backed nylon pan scourer
 2 ft. $\frac{1}{4}$ ins. dowelling
 1 Medium sized file handle
 Adhesive suitable for use with foam.

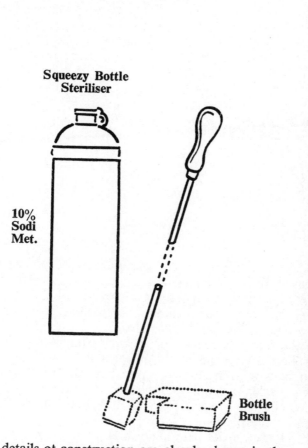

Squeezy Bottle
Steriliser

10%
Sodi
Met.

Bottle
Brush

The details of construction are clearly shown in the
diagram.

CHAPTER 14

Malting

AS grain beer brewers it is essential that we have an appreciation of the basic ingredients for brewing. From the following description of the malting process you will probably appreciate that it is a very delicate and sensitive process and really beyond the scope of the amateur. Unless you are drunk, a thoroughbred purist, or seeking grounds for divorce you will never try and establish yourself as a Home Maltster. In many ways this is a great pity, but I think you will find that it is easier to hand your pennies over the counter to your home-brewer stockist for your Pale Malt rather than try to do-it-yourself.

Barley in its natural form is completely unsuitable for brewing purposes. The basic objects of malting are to convert starch, the major constituent of the grain, into a form where it can be changed into alcohol producing sugars.

Only the finest quality barley is suitable for malting. Inferior grades are malted for the distilling and food industries. Some inferior barley is exported for malting on the Continent where it would be regarded as top quality Lager Malt!

The first part of malting is the steeping process in which the barley grain is soaked in water for a few days to trigger off the growth mechanism of the seedlings.

The barley is then transferred to large malting drums where the growth of the grain is initiated and stimulated by strict temperature and humidity control to achieve optimum germination.

After a few days of germination, the first external signs of growth are visible. Rootlets sprout from the ends of the corn which are encouraged by the natural heat generated by the growth reactions. The higher temperatures can result in too much energy being expanded by the seedling in producing roots at the expense of the final malting extract. A reduction and levelling temperature with constant humidity is achieved by keeping the grain continuously on the move. Drum maltings rotate like giant slow moving cement mixers at a rate of about one revolution per hour. Slow movement is essential to prevent bruising and damage to the delicate seedlings.

Shortly after the appearance of the rootlets from the husks, the rudiments of the future stem can be detected inside the grain. The growth of the stem, called the acrospire, is forced through the grain against the inside of the husk. The length of the acrospire within the husk serves as a useful guide to the degree of modification of the starch to malt. As the shoot extends upwards, the starch is changed into a whiter, looser textured, friable malt flour.

The change is effected by biological catalysts called enzymes, which have the power to initiate chemical reactions of substances in their presence without undergoing any changes in their own structures.

There are many different enzymes in malt formed or activated by the malting processes and which carry out definite functions. The conversion to malt is mainly the responsibility of cytase, and a group of enzymes called the proteolytic enzymes. Cultivation of these enzymes is the concern of the Maltster. The brewer, on the other hand, is more interested in the diatase enzymes which have the power to change this malt flour to fermentable sugar.

The growth of the seedling is allowed to progress until the acrospire is just under two thirds of the length of the grain. Acrospire lengths shorter and larger than this are referred to as "under" and "over" modified malts respectively. Both cases result in a loss of malting extract.

119

Sometimes the yield is purposely sacrificed to retain or restrict other characteristics. Continental Lager malt is under modified and retains the high enzymatic activity, whereas malt for English mashing systems is fully modified to reduce the haze-forming protein matter.

The final section of the malting process is the kiln drying which terminates germination and dries the malt ready for storage. Extra care must be taken in the drying to preserve the enzymatic action and develop the colour of the malt to the required degree. The initial temperature of the drying air should not exceed about 90°F when the grain is still moist. Once the bulk of the moisture has been expelled, the temperature can be raised to between 140° and 160°F depending on the type of malt being made.

Low temperature kilning is favourable for Lager malt where it is essential to preserve the light colour. The side effect of retaining the high enzymatic activity is also particularly beneficial in the decoction method of mashing used in making this beer.

Next up the scale is Pale Malt, which can be regarded as the "normal" malt for mashing and constitutes the bulk proportion of fermentable extract used for English top fermenting ales.

The darker coloured malts, such as Mild Ale, Brown and Amber Malts are roasted to give a high coloured malt and are used in the production of Milds, Browns and Stouts. The latter two malts are little used today, since they contain very little diastatic activity, and their colouring and flavouring abilities can be surpassed by other types of roasted grain.

After the kilning process, which usually lasts up to two days, the dry, brittle redundant rootlets are separated by large sieves to leave just the malted grain.

If the above processes have been carried out successfully, each grain will have lost about a fifth of its original weight. A fair test of the efficiency of malting is to throw about a hundred grains into a bowl of water. Properly malted grains float lengthways on the surface. Poorly malted grains float upright with the end of the grain protruding through the surface of the water. Unmalted grain, on the other hand, just sinks to the bottom.

As the specific gravity of the malt corn is greater than

water, it would seem natural that the reverse results should apply to the above test, i.e. properly malted grains would sink in the water. The difference is due to a small pocket of air trapped in the properly malted grain which aids buoyancy.

An interesting side effect of this phenomenon is that old time brewers did not find it advantageous to purchase malt by weight alone. The brewing measure is a bushel, a volumetric measure, equivalent to a capacity of eight gallons. A bushel of good barley malt should weigh between 41 and 43 lb. The need for rationalisation, however, has now standardised the bushel for barley malt at 42 lb.

Tighter analytical control and measurement of extract and nitrogen content nowadays means that the performance of the malt in the subsequent brewing processes can be assessed with a fair degree of accuracy.

As an amateur, with no real means of analytical assessment of my Pale Malt, I find it gratifying and creditable to the skill of modern day Maltsters, that I rarely come across a bad sample of malt for making my grain beers.

CHAPTER 15

Crushing the malt

THE extract-forming constituents of malt must be exposed to hot water to activate the dormant starch converting enzymes. To facilitate this, the malt has to be crushed or cracked to release its powdery contents. At first thoughts it seems a very simple and ordinary task, but in fact it has to be carried out to very exacting limits to get the best results.

The easiest way over the problem is to buy the Pale Malt already crushed. It does cost approximately 1p more than the whole grain, but for most people, and especially newcomers, it is a worthwhile investment.

Do not try to do it yourself by laying a nylon bag full of malt on the kitchen floor and thumping it with a mallet. The amount of floury dust given off has got to be seen to be believed! Other "man-u-matic" devices such as rollers and mincers can only be regarded as slimming and muscle building exercises, and are therefore not really compatible with the ideals of most home-brewers. Electric coffee grinders are quite often used for cracking malt, but it would be sensible to make a trial brew to prove the quality of crushing.

By studying the specification for cracked malt it is easy for most handymen to make a malt crusher. Obviously, uncracked malt is undesirable since it represents a direct loss of extract. Finely ground malt is the biggest problem, since it tends to "ball" and choke the action of the enzymes. Starch is completely unfermentable by yeast and it is essential that it is completely converted to sugar in the mashing process. Minute traces of unconverted starch, if passed on to the boiling stage, will cause a permanent and irreversible haze in the finished beer. Conversion is most efficient when the malt flour is intermingled and broken up by the husks of grain. By powdering the husks the benefit is lost.

After the mashing process has converted all the starch, the sugars are washed away by rinsing the grain with hot water. The finely ground flour and husks form a paste which "clogs" the filtering process and results in a tiresome condition known as a "set mash".

Home-made grain crusher

My malt crusher is a home-made affair built around the grinding mechanism taken from a hand operated coffee mill. In its original intact form the coffee mill would give a perfect crush to any sized Pale Malt, and really its only real disad-

vantage was in the time and effort expended in processing large quantities of grain. Being lazy, I pitched all my ingenuity into automating the system. The result was the contraption shown in the diagram, which will crush malt at the rate of a pound per minute.

Basically, the grinding mechanism is driven by an electric drill clamped to two wood pillar supports and the whole grain is fed to the crushing wheel via the top half of a funnel. The crushed grain is collected in a plastic bucket. Another section of wood is screwed on the underside of the base, and shaped to give a push fit fixing to the bucket rim to make the receiver dust proof.

If you wish to grind your own malt, then I hope that this arrangement will give you some useful ideas. As yet the trade has not caught up with our needs in this respect, but who knows, in years to come, some enterprising firm may bring an attachment to fit an electric drill that will obviate my efforts.

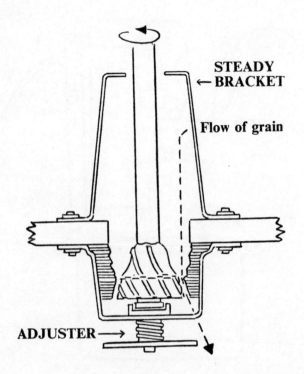

STEADY
← BRACKET

Flow of grain

ADJUSTER →

CHAPTER 16

Mashing

The theory of mashing

THE main extract yielding constituents of malt are starch and cellulose products which are not fermentable by brewing yeasts.

During the mashing process, the infusion of malt and liquor produces a starch solution and frees the enzyme diastase. Enzymes, which control the complex changes in all living matter, act in this case as a catalyst to bring about a simultaneous chemical reaction that reduces the starch to fermentable sugar. The diastase converts the starch into a mixture of sugars grouped as dextrins and maltose. Dextrins are less fermentable than maltose.

Maltose is readily accepted by the yeast and ferments rapidly, whereas the dextrins possess restrictive properties that make them respond more slowly.

Enzymes

The name diastase is the collective grouping of two separate enzymes: alpha and beta amylase. It is the response of these two enzymes to the temperature of the mash, and the physical environment within the mash-tun, that decides the proportion of maltose to dextrin.

The trend of response to temperature and pH of the mash is similar for both, but the peaks and operating parameters are different.

Alpha amylase is chiefly responsible for breaking down the starch to dextrinous sugars that give no colour on an iodine test. The enzyme has a high thermal stability and can withstand temperatures greater than what would normally be experienced in the mash-tun. Optimum conditions for alpha amylase are experienced at 149°F at a pH 5·7.

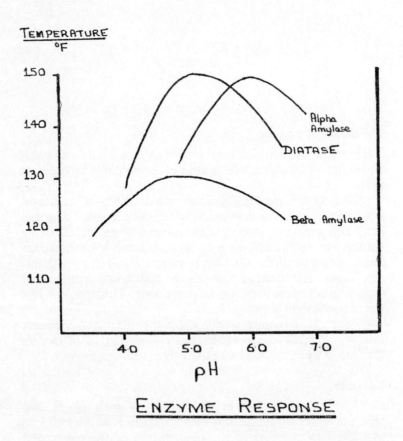

ENZYME RESPONSE

Beta amylase is the more delicate enzyme of the two, and possesses the ability to break starch down directly, or indirectly via dextrins, to the readily fermentable maltose. In the mash-tun its main source of energy is expended in just simplifying the dextrins to maltose; the dextrins having been produced by the action of the alpha enzyme. Optimum operating conditions are at 131°F at a pH of 4·7.

In the mash-tun the action of alpha and beta amylase cannot be separated, hence conditions of temperature and acidity must be selected to give the most satisfactory compromise. This is basically why their action is grouped as diastase, which is most effective at 150°F at a pH of 5·1.

Under these conditions, the wort will yield approximately 25 per cent dextrins and 75 per cent maltose, which makes an ideal balance for our English beers made with the infusion mash system.

Mash reactions

A lower mashing heat produces excessive maltose and insufficient dextrin, and a higher mash temperature produces excessive dextrins at the expense of the maltose. A few degrees either way from the optimum of 150°F can cause striking differences in attenuation characteristics and limiting gravities of the beer.

The restrictive properties on fermentation of dextrins make them invaluable for providing the conditioning gas in the bottle or barrel, hence, long maturing, high gravity ales are mashed at 152–154°F to ensure an ample supply of these sugars.

Quick maturing beers, such as Mild Ale, require the extra maltose that can be supplied by mashing at 147–149°F.

The critical period of mashing is in the first few minutes, when the enzymes are shocked into activity by the hot liquor. The water used for the infusion is usually designed to be about 20°F higher than the mash temperature to allow for the cooling effect of the dry grain. The grain takes in heat as it absorbs water, raising its temperature up to the required value and also it reduces the temperature of the water to the same value. An intimate mix should ensure an even temperature throughout the mash.

Inefficient initial mixing can result in sections or pockets of grain being exposed to very hot water. The beta amylase enzyme just cannot tolerate high temperatures (160–170°F). If a marked reduction in temperature is not forthcoming within a few minutes, this poor enzyme is scalded to destruction. The loss of this enzyme will over burden the alpha component and will increase the likelihood of an incomplete conversion.

Between 150° and 154°F the enzymes are extremely active so long as the acidity of the mash is correct. The higher temperatures encourage enzyme performance as well as accelerating the destruction of beta amylase. Thus, if incorrect acidity prolongs the starch conversion time, then again trouble can be experienced. So with the higher mash temperatures, checking and correcting the pH is essential. With ideal mash conditions starch end point should be passed within 30 minutes.

Beginners to mashing techniques should aim for the initial temperature of 150°F with the acidity adjusted to a pH of 5·0–5·3. The starch in the grain should be completely changed to sugar within 45 minutes. This means that all the starch has been at least converted to dextrin. Some dextrin will be further reduced to maltose, but this is of no consequence in the iodine test. Conversion to dextrins is always completed before the maximum amount of maltose is produced, and hence it is the former reaction that is being monitored. At Starch End Point for these optimum conditions, the wort contains approximately 40 per cent maltose and 60 per cent dextrins.

In real terms, if a beer was brewed with this wort with say a starting gravity of 50, then the fermentation would abate at an SG of around 30. The beer would be a sickly, sweet, malty mess, completely lacking in balance.

Obviously, this state of affairs is intolerable, and hence a further breakdown of the dextrins is necessary. In practice, the mash is allowed to stand for another 1–1½ hours after saccharification of the mash to allow the enzymes to reduce more of the dextrins to fermentable maltose. The prolonged rest results in correct balance, but in achieving this end, again most of the beta amylase is destroyed.

Beta amylase stands a much better chance of survival

by mashing a few degrees lower than 150°F. Alpha activity is correspondingly subdued, and thus Starch End Point may take considerably longer to pass. From my experience, about 1 hour would seem to be about the average under these conditions. By the time the iodine test gives a positive approval of zero starch, the maltose content may be as high as 60 per cent. A further rest will increase this figure by about another 20 per cent.

Another important reaction taking place simultaneously with the starch conversion is the reduction of nitrogenous matter. The major cause of defects in brilliance in bacterially stable beer is due to the clouding from nitrogenous substances. Proteins are the main offender in this category. A certain amount of protein digestion is carried out in the malting stage to minimise this problem, especially with our English malts.

The barley proteins are grouped as Albumin, Globulin, Gliadin and Gutelin, but it is only the first two that can justify our amateur attention.

During mashing, enzymes, proteinase and sometimes peptidase progressively break down the proteins into amino acids and other simpler lower molecular weight substances. The extent of this degradation is dependent on the mash temperature and pH. For each protein there is a particular pH value at which the breakdown (proteolysis) process is a maximum. Thus, for one mash pH value, it is impossible to fully degrade all the protein matter.

Fortunately mashing at a pH of around 5·0 results in near maximum digestion of the haze forming fraction of globulin (beta globulin), but at the same time retaining a good measure of the head retention products derived from the breakdown of Albumin. The proteolytic action in the mash-tun degrades some of these proteins which were initially insoluble into nitrogenous substances that are permanently soluble in wort.

The enzyme peptidase cannot survive in the normal infusion mash temperatures (145–155°F) and thus protein digested is somewhat restricted, but nevertheless, it is usually sufficient to deal with well modified English malts. High nitrogen malts therefore present difficulties for infusion mashing and sometimes a preliminary low temperature mash must be included to reap the benefit of the peptidase enzyme. Continental decoction mash systems are an example of this reasoning.

The effect of pH

All the brewing processes are just as vulnerable to change in pH as they are to temperature.

At mixing, the pH of the strike liquor will fall dramatically as the liquid forms a dilute solution of acid through reaction with the malt phosphates.

Recommended pH values are:—

Top Fermenting Beers pH 5·0–5·1
Bottom Fermenting Beers pH 5·3–5·6

Top fermenting ales are typically more attenuative than the bottom fermenting varieties, as is reflected by the pH values. Lower pH values favour the production of readily fermentable maltose, and the higher figures the slow maturing dextrins. The latter suits the long storage times of Lager.

The nature of the mashing water has an important influence on the mash reactions. Carbonate liquors, due to their alkalinity, will buffer the enzyme reactions away from the recommended values unless the pH is restored by Dark Malts. Gypseous waters are generally beneficial for light beers. The effect of water treatment on these reactions, though, is more fully discussed in other chapters.

Stiffness of the mash

There is a very interesting physical side effect of mashing. The enzymes don't get on very well together! Consequently, the amount of hot water used to intimately mix these constituents is rather critical. Initially, a stiff mash is beneficial in initiating the reactions that produce sugars, but, when the starch is reduced to dextrins, the action of these sugars oppose the efforts of the maltose producing enzyme, beta amylase. Similarly, maltose restricts the action of alpha amylase, so if we are not careful, the enzymes chase themselves around in circles, and finally disappear in a cloud of amolytic frenzy!

Practically, dilution of the mash after saccharification benefits the subsequent breakdown of sugars by giving the

130

enzymes more room to react. Our systems of mashing, especially the insulated mash-tuns, experience a slight fall in temperature towards saccharification, so that restoring the mash temperature by adding very hot water serves two useful purposes at the same time.

Dilute mashes favour the production of maltose and stiff mashes produce more dextrins.

THE BREWER'S BEDTIME STORY

"Saccharomyces and the Two Enzymes"

The complex theory of mashing regarding the breakdown of malt starch to fermentable sugar can be illustrated better by my Brewer's Bedtime Story about the Starch Tree Forest, and the enzymes that live in it.

If you are sitting comfortably, then I will begin!

Alf and Betty Amylase were a couple of very nice enzymes from the Diastase family, living in the suburbs of Grain Husks, who made their living by working in the Starch Tree Forests that surrounded their homestead. By chopping down the trees it was possible to make firewood for building fires to keep their small son, Saccharomyces, warm and healthy. Saccharomyces was a growing lad, and his parents found that the work in the forest was a full-time job.

It was an arduous existence, demanding the co-operation of both parents. Each morning they would go out into the forest, Alf taking his big chopper, and Betty the small kindling knife.

The routine for the day was simple. Before any work commenced they both sat down and enjoyed a hot cup of coffee. Feeling refreshed, big strong Alf would then start to chop down the starch trees.

As soon as the first log was chopped off, Betty would immediately start to slice it into small pieces called maltose sticks, thus allowing Alf to carry on chopping the next log. Betty was an industrious wife, but she found that it was impossible to slice the logs up at the same rate as Alf was supplying them. She did her best to cope with the ever increasing pile of dextrin logs.

The most important stage to be attained, as far as they were concerned, was the complete dissection of the starch trees into dextrin logs. Dextrin logs would at least burn, whereas the whole tree could never be coaxed into flame, no matter how many boxes of matches were used.

Alf and Betty referred to this juncture as the Starch End Point—the stage where the non-inflammable tree was reduced to a usable fuel.

Working at their normal rate, by the time Alf had cut down the whole tree into dextrin logs, his wife had been able to slice almost half of them into maltose sticks.

From experience, the fire needed to be constructed from both logs and sticks, and the most efficient combination was a quarter logs and three-quarters sticks. Each bundle of maltose sticks would quickly catch alight and burn furiously to expend its heat energy in a very short space of time. The inclusion of a quarter of logs gave the fire "body" and it also assisted by filling the valleys of inactivity between successive bundles of maltose.

At Starch End Point, all the wood was "burnable", but unfortunately, at this juncture, the ratio between logs and sticks did not create the best conditions for a healthy fire. The high proportion of logs meant that the fire would smoulder rather than roar into life.

The job of breaking down some of the remaining logs into maltose sticks to create a better balance was mainly the responsibility of Betty.

Alf's chopper was so large and unwieldy that it was a difficult task for him to chop the logs into minute sticks. He did try to do this once on his own, but it took the best part of two days to complete one tree. Similarly, Betty could not really be expected to slice the Starch Tree into maltose sticks with her small knife, without Alf first cutting the tree down into manageable units. It was *possible*, but in both cases, it was much better to work as a team to tackle the job.

The efficiency of the team was always very sensitive to the weather conditions; especially temperature. The hotter the day became, the faster Alf and Betty worked. Betty, however, found that she could not sustain the increased work rate, and after a while, her contribution diminished somewhat. Alf still produced the logs, but Betty just could not slice up so many of them into sticks. If the temperature rose too high, Betty would faint and leave Alf to do all the work himself.

132

The result was to reduce the number of sticks available for the fire, thus diminishing the heat output.

In colder weather the situation was reversed, since they both had to put on warm heavy clothing. Betty, nevertheless, could quite happily sit slicing up the logs without a reduction in her performance. Alf, though, found that the heavy clothing impeded his movement and his swing with the chopper. The restriction was such ar to reduce the number of logs he could chop. His rate would be so slow that Betty could now keep up with him and slice each log into sticks as soon as they became available.

The moral of this story, then, is: Create the best working conditions for the team, taking fully into consideration the individual preferences of the participating workers, and channel their efforts to the best advantage of the process.

Can you relate the cast to their equivalent roles in brewing? We have the Alpha and Beta Enzymes represented by Alf and Betty, the grains of Pale Malt by the Starch Trees, the dextrins and maltose sugars by the logs and sticks, and the "fermentability" of the wort by the "burnability" of the fuel.

The story can b. related further into the brewing processes, for instance, the amount of water used in the mix is equivalent to the size of the clearing in the forest, their working area, and so on.

This simple simile is a useful aid in creating a mental picture to provide a tangible explanation of the complex theory. No doubt you can continue the story to suit your own ideas of the brewing processes.

Preparing the grist

The grist, as the mixture of dry grain is called, should be weighed in the proportion recommended in the recipe. With Pale Malt and all extract bearing whole grains, the degree of crushing is of paramount importance and ideally the result should just consist of the whole halves of husks and the powdery interiors. With Crystal, Black and Roast Malts, the degree of crushing is not so critical, and any means that will expose the insides for extraction in the mash-tun will be suitable. Flaked adjuncts can be mixed directly with the rest of the crushed grain. Mixing should ideally be carried out in a separate container to the mash-tun, such as a two-gallon plastic bucket.

Thorough mixing of the grist is essential to ensure an even dispersion of the non-enzyme-bearing adjuncts. The grist should be "scoop-mixed" rather than stirred. Mixing is best effected by attempting to scoop the grain from the bottom of the container to the top. In this manner, separation of the malt flour from the husks is prevented, which would otherwise cause the flour to sieve through the husks and form a layer at the bottom. Flour not broken up by grain husks increases the tendency for mash to "set" and clog.

Preparing the mashing liquor

The mashing liquor should be treated as necessary considering the type of beer and the nature of the dissolved solids. Typical range for strike heats for our mash-tuns are:—

Insulated Mash-Tuns (preheated)   165–168°F
Floating Mash-Tuns (unheated)   168–172°F

To give an ample reserve, a minimum of 3 pints of water should be prepared for each pound of grist. The floating mash-tun principle inherently satisfies these requirements. It is always preferable to raise the temperature of the strike liquor about 10°F above the required values, and let it cool down to the correct value. A more even distribution of heat is achieved this way.

The range of strike heats quoted above allow for the slight difference in the physical characteristics of the equipment and also for allowances in the stiffness of the mash. Stiff mashes need higher strike heats than dilute mashes.

Preparing the mash-tun

The insulated mash-tun should be pre-heated before use, to ensure that the container does not soak away too much heat from the mash. By raising the temperature of the inside of the mash-tun to mash heat, the loss of essential heat is prevented. A thermometer in a brass tube can be suspended in the water, to check stabilisation; the string being jammed in position by the lid. Ten minutes of this treatment should be sufficient, after which the water should be thrown away if it is not going to be used for mashing. Although wasteful,

I prefer to discard this water, so that I can use some more which can be added, and mixed to the grain in small but frequent stages. Adding the grain to the water increases the thermal shock to the sensitive enzymes, but in practice, I have not found that this causes any problems.

After the preliminary heat treatment for the insulated tun, the subsequent preparations are similar. The tap of the mash-tun should be checked, cleaned and closed before the false bottom and grain bag are placed in position. The grain bag must rest on the false bottom, and the surplus mesh at the top is folded back over the rim of the container.

Mashing

The mash-tun is then placed, if possible, beneath the tap of the boiler, and the mashing liquor allowed to flow in until the false bottom is just covered.

The dry grist can now be ladled in, stirring slowly, but positively, with a wooden spoon to ensure an even mix that is devoid of any dry spots. More grain and more water can now be added, ensuring that the mixture maintains a porridge-like consistency. At about the half way stage check the temperature of the "goods", as the mixture is now known, to confirm that it is settling out to between 150 and 152°F. Give the goods another quick stir and test the temperature in another position to reaffirm the first reading. It is surprising how often there is a discrepancy, and the mash must, if this happens, be stirred until the readings are the same. Readings outside the narrow 2°F range can be dealt with in the mixing of the second portion of grist. Temperatures below 150°F will require the consistency of the following mix to be much thinner and more diluted. Higher temperatures necessitate reducing the ratio of the mixing water to give a stiffer mash.

When all the grain has been mixed in, the level of water should ideally just cover the surface of the goods. Again the temperature must be checked after stirring and must this time be adjusted to 150°F using boiling or cold water. It is far more important to achieve the correct temperature than it is to worry about the dilution of the mash. The boiled water should be at hand prior to the mixing of the grist.

136

Checking and adjusting pH

With the temperature correct, dip in a slip of pH paper for an acidity check. Place the wet slip on a white saucer to reflect the true shade of the colour change. A pH between 5·0 and 5·5 is our goal. High values indicate insufficient acidity, which can usually be rectified by cautiously adding Calcium or Magnesium Salts to the hot infusion. Calcium Carbonate will produce the opposite effect.

The thermometer and wooden spoon can be left in the goods, sufficiently immersed not to impede the fitting of the lid.

Now that the physical and chemical conditions have been checked and found correct, the mashing process should be allowed to progress without further interruption.

The insulated mash-tun can be replaced in its original stout cardboard box packaging for extra lagging and allowed to rest in a warm, draught-free position. A large towel can be placed over the lid to reduce this major source of heat loss.

For the second method, the polythene bucket type mash-tun (see chapter 5), should be transferred and allowed to float in the boiler water. Be very careful with this operation as an accident with this exposed heavy hot container could be very nasty. The temperature of the boiler water would be maintained between 165 and 145°F for the duration of the mashing period. Actually, the temperature of water should still be about 165–170°F from the time that some of the water was drawn off as mashing liquor. The boiler can be switched off, since the thermal inertia of the arrangement is adequate to maintain the goods temperature in the mash-tun constant for at least the saccharification period. Over a two to three hour mash, I find that the boiler temperature only needs boosting once. The heat gradually emits from the boiler and when the temperature falls to about 145°F, I switch it on again to raise the temperature back to about 165°F.

Mashing overnight

The mashing process takes a minimum of two hours. My simple methods have been purposely designed so that once

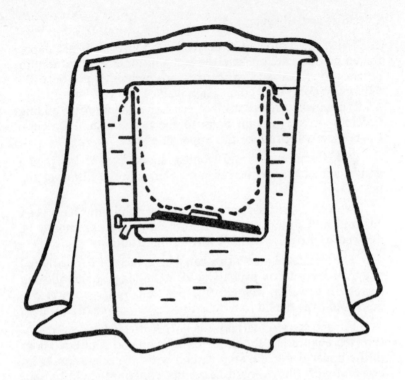

the process has been started, the apparatus can be left completely unattended until the grain has "mashed itself".

The testing for Starch End Point and diluting the mash after saccharification need not necessarily be carried out if certain conditions are observed.

Probably three-quarters of my brews are made by carrying over the mashing process overnight. After all, if the mashing process is capable of looking after itself, why should we interfere? The long period of mashing seems to produce a more efficient reaction and better extraction. Eight to ten hours will certainly give the enzymes full opportunity to digest and convert every little speck of starch.

The effect of a long mash must be considered. Firstly, the leisurely manner of mashing will enable the enzymes to reduce more of the dextrin "logs" into highly fermentable "maltose" sticks which would inevitably produce a thin beer lacking in fullness of palate. To offset this problem, all that

138

is necessary is to just start the mashing process a few degrees higher than the optimum (say 152°F) to encourage the production of more dextrins. This is easily achieved by adding more hot water than usual. In adding more water conveniently satisfies the other recommendation of diluting the mash after saccharification.

The whole sequence fits neatly into place like a jig-saw puzzle, to make these methods so simple and workable. Extra insulation is recommended for an overnight mash. An old blanket or a large towel draped over the equipment will just provide that extra bit of insulation. The temperature of the grain within the mash will fall to between 130 and 120°F overnight which is perfectly acceptable for this technique.

Testing for starch

It is advisable to check the progress of the reactions in mashing by testing a sample of the grains for the presence of starch. When mashing within a degree or two of 150°F, the malt enzymes should have converted the starch in the grain into a form of sugar within the first three-quarters of an hour.

To test for starch, remove a teaspoonful of the mashed grain and liquor from the mash-tun, and place it on a white saucer or tile. Using an eyedropper, add a few drops of Tincture of Iodine to the sample. The brown iodine solution will immediately darken the grain mixture to a deep, bluish-black colour if there is starch present. A predominance of blackened grains is sometimes an indication of poorly crushed malt. All samples must be discarded after testing, and the test gear washed clean before any further checks are made.

If this colour reaction still persists with samples taken after 1–1¼ hours, then mashing is not progressing as would be anticipated. Check the temperature and reaffirm the pH value. High temperatures may kill off the beta amylase prematurely, making it difficult to complete the mash reaction. In this instance, the temperature must be lowered to between 140 and 150°F, and a cupful of crushed pale malt grains stirred in to provide additional enzymes for converting the remaining unfermentable starch. Diastatic malt extract syrups can also be usefully employed for this duty.

Low temperature mashes not yielding a positive test within this time, are often the result of an incorrect mash pH.

Simply adjust the figure back to the recommended value: the enzyme activity should still be adequate for the job.

Where both temperature and pH are correct, the mash will require some dilution to give the enzymes more room to work.

When all the starch is converted to sugar, the iodine added to the sample of grains will not change colour. This condition is referred to as the Starch End Point. Under no circumstances must this conjuncture be regarded as the completion of mashing. The malt sugars must always, with grain beers, be broken down further to achieve a better balanced wort.

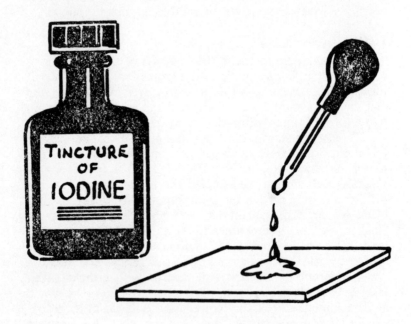

CHAPTER 17

Sparging

THE object of sparging is to rinse out the viscous sticky sugars from the husks of the grain after mashing.

The separation of the sweet wort from the redundant husks makes the subsequent treatment much easier. Just imagine the mess it would make of your boiler or kitchen stove if you tried to boil the large sticky mass of grains with the hops and sugar!

Sugar, when in solution, will flow much more easily and readily when it is hot. Sweet wort is no exception, and the whole theory of sparging is based on this principle. Ideally, it would be nice if all the hot sweet wort would drain naturally from the spent grain. In practice, though, about 40 per cent of the extract could be retrieved in this manner. Some of the spent half sections of grain husks act as "cups" that fill with hot wort and retain the extract within the mash-tun. During sparging, other pieces of husks which are upside down, act as umbrellas to the downward flow of sparge water and shield the extract from being washed away towards the tap. The physical disposition of grain husks must to a large extent be accepted and not disturbed. Stirring up the mash to reverse the roles of the "cups" and "umbrellas" must only be resorted to if the extract cannot be retrieved by the standard methods of approach.

The necessity is due to the fact that the grain still contains finely divided matter, which if washed out with the wort, could cause problems with clarity, stability, and flavour of the beer. The grain husks give porosity to the mash and drainage for the wort. By gentle packing, due to their natural weight, the husks also act as a filter for these undesirable substances, and hence any agitation of the mash could possibly have serious consequences.

The efficiency of sparging can be gauged by the amount of water that is needed to extract all the fermentable matter. I suppose really that sparging could be summed up by saying that the object is to extract the maximum amount of sugar using the minimum amount of water.

Sparging fifty gallons of water through five gallons of mashed grain would certainly extract the sugar, but the beer brewed from it would be weak, virtually tasteless, colourless and non-alcoholic.

Average strength beers require the mashed extract to make up about 30–40 degrees of the starting specific gravity. Thus allowing for the raising of specific gravity due to evaporation during boiling, the gravity of the collected wort after sparging should at least have a specific gravity of 25. Therefore, this means that the sparge water must be limited to a maximum of one gallon of water for every pound of mashed grain. More water than this will inevitably call for a prolonged boil which would be time-consuming and awkward.

The degree of crushing of the malt has an important bearing on the efficiency of sparging. Too fine a crush will cause the powdered husks to cake on to the mesh of the grain bag and block the flow of sparged wort. In these circumstances, the grain must be stirred to clear the blockage and allowed to stand for a few minutes before sparging recommences. Bad cases, however, will block almost immediately again and the treatment must be repeated. This is a tiresome condition, and once you have experienced it, I am sure that you will do your utmost to make certain that it does not happen again.

Running off the wort

Armed with the background knowledge of the process, and its requirements and pitfalls, it is possible to implement it practically.

quantity below the false bottom. The space acts as a settling tank and the wort will thus contain large amounts of debris which could be injurious to the quality of the beer.

A rough test for the efficiency of sparging is to taste a sample of the spent grains. No sugar should be detected if sparging has been carried out correctly.

The spent grains can then be discarded. Around my back garden there are numerous mounds of spent grain from successive brews. The grains seem to attract all the worms in the neighbourhood, which I suppose, in my ignorance in these matters, is good for the soil. My wife, who is the gardener in the household, has threatened that if one small blade of barley is seen to grow from these mounds, I shall be in trouble!

CHAPTER 18

The hydrometer

THE Hydrometer is an essential instrument for a home-brewer to have in his brewery. Known originally as a Saccharometer and affectionally termed "the Brewer's Compass", it gives an unerring guide to the efficiency of mashing and the progress of fermentation. The word "saccharometer" actually means "a measure of sweetness".

When the hydrometer is placed in water at a temperature of 60°F it sinks until the surface of the water cuts the stem at the point marked 0 (Zero). Wort, the liquid extract drawn from malt after its infusion in hot water, is a mixture of sugar and water and is heavier than water alone. When placed in this wort the hydrometer will only partially sink. The distance between the point where the wort cuts the stem of the hydrometer and that when it is placed in plain water is proportional to the amount of sugar in the wort. The richer the wort the higher the hydrometer will float.

The hydrometer thus indicates how much heavier a wort or sugar solution is than water, and is calibrated in degrees of gravity. The word "gravity" means weight. Thus the greater the density of the wort, the greater will be its weight and the hydrometer shows the additional weight in excess of water.

For example, 1 lb. of sugar dissolved in water to give a total volume of 1 gal. weighs 1·0375 times as much as 1 gal. of pure water. The point where the sugar solution cuts the stem of the hydrometer is marked at 37·5 and is known as a specific gravity of 37·5, or abbreviated again to read SG of 37·5. With 2 lb. of sugar in 1 gal. the hydrometer will float higher in the solution at a point marked 75, and so on. Intermediate readings are directly proportional to the sugar content.

The other important use of the hydrometer is in checking the progress of fermentation. At the start of fermentation the gravity of the wort is high (averaging between S.G. 40 and S.G. 60). By means of fermentation a great part of the malt sugar in the wort is changed to alcohol which is less dense than water. As the alcohol is formed the wort is attenuated, that is, becomes lighter, and the hydrometer sinks further down in the wort and the reading falls. By subtracting the final gravity reading from the initial one, it is therefore possible to calculate how much alcohol has been produced. Dividing the "gravity" drop or difference by 7·46 gives the alcohol content by volume (v/v).

Example

To find the alcohol content of a beer with a starting specific gravity of 50, and a final specific gravity of 10.

Then, from the graph, the starting gravity of 50 could produce 6·7 per cent of alcohol, but the beer attenuation is arrested at a S.G. of 10, showing that the final 1·3 per cent of alcohol will not be produced.

Hence, the alcohol in the beer, $= 6·7 - 1·3$

$$= 5·4\%$$

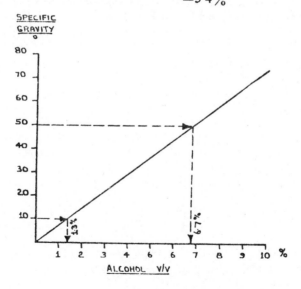

Effect of temperature

The specific gravity reading varies considerably with temperature. When a liquid, such as wort, is heated, its volume expands and thus it becomes less dense. A Hydrometer placed in this liquid will therefore gradually sink as the temperature rises and the specific gravity falls. To create a standard, Hydrometers are calibrated at a temperature of 60°F. All references to gravity in this book are also to this standard. Corrections can be made as follows:—

Degrees drop 0	10	20	30	40	50	60	70	80	90
Alcohol % V 0	1	2	3	4	5	6	7	8	9	10

Temperature	50	59	70	80	90	100	110
× Reading by	0.98	1.00	1.02	1.05	1.11	1.22	1.36
Temperature	120	130	140	150	160	170	
× Reading by	1.52	1.70	1.92	2.15	2.42	2.75	

Example

At 130°F, a sample indicated a S.G. of 20. The correction factor from the table for 130°F is 1·70.

Then, the true reading corrected to 60°F $= 20 \times 1\cdot70$

$$\text{S.G.} = 34$$

CHAPTER 19

Degrees of extract

THE commercial trade quote the extract from malt in terms of Brewers Pounds per Quarter, a peculiar measurement steeped in tradition and devised in the times when the extract could only be checked by the weight of the extracted sugar. Sugar is heavier than water, and thus a volume of sugar solution will weigh more than the same volume of plain water. Wort is a solution of Malt Sugar, and Brewers Pounds refer to the excess weight of a barrel of wort over a barrel of water. Really, this is all a hydrometer indicates when it floats in wort. Thank goodness for science in the form of this small glass instrument. If this simple device was not available, we would still have to resort to checking the gravity of the wort by weight.

Just imagine the procedure involved in carting your five gallon dustbin of beer each morning to the bathroom scales to weigh it to check the progress of fermentation. It would be far easier to recalibrate the scales in degrees of specific gravity to save some lengthy calculations. I don't think though, that your wife would be very pleased to learn that she weighs the same as ten gallons of your best bitter!

Typical extracts for Pale Malt quoted by the Malting Companies is currently between 101 and 103 Brewers Pounds per Quarter.

Brewers Pounds refer to the excess weight of a barrel of wort over that of a barrel of water. A barrel of water weighs:

$$36 \text{ gallons} \times 10 \text{ lb./gallon} = 360 \text{ lb.}$$

Considering the average extract figure of 102 Brewers Pounds, means that if all the sugar extracted from one quarter (336 lb.) of malt were dissolved in 1 barrel, the weight of the solution would be:—

$$360+102=462 \text{ lb.}$$

The relative gravity $= \dfrac{462}{360} = 1 \cdot 283$

The specific gravity $= 283°$ for the 36 gallons.

Now to find the specific gravity of the extract from 1 lb. of this malt in 1 gal. (or 336 lb. in 336 gallons) the above solution would have to be diluted 36/336 times.

Hence Specific Gravity $= 283 \times \dfrac{36}{336} = 30 \cdot 3°$

102 Brewers Pounds/Quarter=Specific Gravity 30·3 per lb./gallon.

TABLE 1

Brewers pounds	S.G.
60	17·8
70	20·7
80	23·7
90	26·7
95	28·2
100	29·7
101	30·0
102	30·3
103	30·6
104	30·9
105	31·2

Typical extract figures for our common brewing ingredients are:

TABLE 2

Fermentable sugar	Brewers pounds	Degrees of extract (Specific Gravity 1 lb. per gallon)
Pale malt	100–103	29·7–30·6
Lager malt	100–103	29·7–30·6
Crystal malt	80	23·7
Flaked barley	100–105	29·7–31·2
Flaked rice	100–105	29·7–31·2
Flaked maize	100–105	29·7–31·2
White sugar	125	37·5
Demerara sugar	120	36·0
Invert sugar	102	30·3
Malt extract	102	30·3

To be candid, I find the commercial breweries' ideas of expressing extract unnecessarily complicated.

The method I have used for years seems so obvious and easy that I am surprised that nobody, as far as I know, has used it as a standard approach for determining the extract from these ingredients.

The system is based on the weight or equivalent weight of sugar that these carbohydrates will yield in solution. Instead of measuring in terms of pounds and ounces, I relate the weight in terms of degrees of specific gravity produced in 1 gallon.

The bulk of fermentables in all beers must be derived from Pale Malt grains. From table 2 it can be seen that 1 pound of good malt should yield a specific gravity of 30 for 1 gallon of wort. For my system then, I calculate extract in terms of Degrees of Specific Gravity. That is, for Pale Malt, I say it has an extract of up to 30 degrees. Flaked adjuncts have a slightly higher yield, and roasted malts slightly lower than the Pale Malt. Since these other fermentable grains are used in minor proportions (e.g. 10–15 per cent) I have averaged and rounded off these yields to 30 degrees as well.

By going through a few examples, the versatility of this

151

system is easily shown. Let us assume that we are going to mash 7 lb. of Pale Malt, then the

Maximum Possible Extract = 7 (lb.) × 30 = 210 degrees

This figure has been calculated for all the extract being contained in 1 gallon of wort. An all malt beer having a specific gravity of 210 would be mighty powerful stuff! In practice, a weaker brew would be needed, and if we used this malt to make 4 gallons of beer then the

$$\text{Specific Gravity} = \frac{210 \text{ degrees}}{4 \text{ gallons}} = 52.5°$$

Similarly, for a 5 gallon brew

$$\text{Specific Gravity} = \frac{210 \text{ degrees}}{5 \text{ gallons}} = 42°$$

And again, for a 7 gallon brew

$$\text{Specific Gravity} = \frac{210 \text{ degrees}}{7 \text{ gallons}} = 30°$$

Being able to pre-determine the extract, with due allowances made for your average mash efficiences, is a great help in formulating recipes. The extract from Pale Malt grains fixes the amount of added sugar, hop rate and the gravity and final length of the beer. By determining the practical extract figure obtained after mashing, these figures can be checked before the wort constituents and recipe are fixed permanently by the boiling process.

I regard these simple calculations and checks as an essential procedure to be adopted for making every grain beer brew. The log from my recipe book for "Country Life Bitter" emphasises these points quite well. The basis for the recipe was as follows:—

> 6 lb. Crushed Pale Malt
> ¾ lb. Flaked Maize
> ½ lb. Cracked Crystal Malt

The above grist was mashed for three hours at a temperature ranging between 150 and 145°F. After confirming that Starch End Point had been passed, the goods were sparged with hot water at 170°F to retrieve 6 gallons of wort. The specific gravity for the 6 gallons, corrected to room temperature, was 35. Thus the amount of malt sugar taken from the grain, or

Actual extract = 6 gallons × 35 = 210 *degrees*

The maximum possible extract, or Theoretical Extract, that it would be possible to achieve can be calculated using the data in table 1.

$$
\begin{array}{lll}
\text{Pale Malt} & =6\ \text{lb.}\times30= & 180 \\
\text{Flaked Maize} & =\tfrac{3}{4}\ \text{lb.}\times30= & 21 \\
\text{Crystal Malt} & =\tfrac{1}{2}\ \text{lb.}\times30= & \underline{15} \\
& \text{TOTAL}= & 216
\end{array}
$$

Maximum Possible Extract = 216 *Degrees*

From which,

$$\text{Efficiency of Mashing} = \frac{210}{216} \times 100 \text{ per cent} = 97 \text{ per cent}$$

If I had been lazy and reduced the sparging time so that only 5 gallons of wort were collected, then almost certainly some of the malt sugar would have been retained in the spent grains. The specific gravity for the 5 gallons could have been for example, 38 giving a

Actual Extract of 5 gallons × 38 = 190 *degrees*

Thus the

$$\text{Efficiency of Mashing} = \frac{190}{216} \times 100 \text{ per cent} = 88 \text{ per cent}$$

Although this latter figure is based on guesswork, it is near to the efficiency that could be expected for a limited sparging operation. Working from the original extract figures, it was then possible to calculate the rest of the fermentables that were needed as sugar. Since I was trying to produce a full bodied bitter, I deemed it necessary that the

153

grain should provide 80 per cent of the total extract. The sugar then needed to contribute

$$20\% \times \frac{210}{80\%} = 52 \cdot 5 \text{ degrees}$$

Using white sugar, this would be the equivalent to

$$\frac{52 \cdot 5}{37 \cdot 5} = 1 \text{ lb. 6oz.} = \frac{\text{Extract Required}}{\text{Extract for white sugar}}$$

To round off the figures, I decided to use 1½ lb. of white sugar in the brew. The contribution to the extract was therefore 1½ lb. ×37·5=56·5 degrees. Combining this figure with the mashed extract, the total fermentable extract that was at my disposal was

Total Fermentable Extract = 210 + 56·5 = 266·5 *degrees*

The 6 gallons of wort were then boiled with the sugar 3 ozs. of Goldings hops for 1¼ hr. After the boil, the quantity of wort strained off the spent hops had been reduced to 5 gallons. The gravity was again checked and found to be 52, which at the time seemed about the right figure.

It was only after the brew had been pitched with a top fermenting yeast that I decided to calculate exactly what the starting gravity should have been, i.e.

$$\text{Theoretical Starting Gravity} = \frac{\text{Total Fermentable Extract}}{\text{Final Volume}} = \frac{266 \cdot 5}{5 \text{ gallon}} =$$

$$53 \cdot 3 \text{ degrees}$$

The difference of 1·3° represented for the 5 gallons 5 × 1·4°=7 degrees of extract, which from table 2 can be seen to be equivalent to about 3 ozs. of white sugar. This was the extract lost through retention in the spent hops.

The great advantage with knowing the actual total fermentable extract available, is that it is possible to adjust the beer accurately as regards quantity or specific gravity to suit your particular requirements.

154

By topping up the beer to 6 gallons, the starting gravity would have been

$$\frac{\text{Actual Total Extract}}{\text{Final Volume}} = \frac{5 \text{ gallons} \times 52}{\text{Final Volume}} = \frac{260 \text{ degrees}}{6 \text{ gallons}} =$$

$$\text{S.G.} = 43\cdot5 \text{ degrees}$$

Alternatively, if I had wanted the beer to have a starting gravity of 50, then,

$$50° = \frac{\text{Total Extract}}{\text{Required Volume}}$$

$$\text{Required Volume} = \frac{260}{50} = 5\cdot2 \text{ gallons} =$$

5 gallons 1½ pints, approximately, so that 1½ pints of water would be required to be added to the 5 gallons of beer to reduce the S.G. from 52 to 50.

From the above it can be appreciated that the "Degrees of Extract" system can provide a means of sensibly formulating and checking recipes, as well as being a useful tool for quality control. Each stage of the brewing process can be easily checked for efficiency. By testing the gravity of each successive gallon of wort, it is possible to calculate the convenient quantity of sparge water to suit your brewing gear. After all, there is not much point in sparging the grain with an extra gallon of water just to wring out the final few ounces of saccharine matter, if by doing so, it is going to take an extra hour's boiling to restore the diluted wort back to its required value.

Similarly, during the checks in the above sample, it was noticed that 7 degrees of extract were left in the hops after the wort had been strained off. More care with the hop sparge in future brews could possibly reduce this loss.

If the beer and yourself survive the "hard sums", pitch the former with a top fermenting yeast and reward the latter with a pint of best draught Stout. Both will benefit from these respective actions.

Ferment the beer for 4–5 days and then rack off into a polythene cube. Bottle or cask the beer a week later.

I wonder if the above system of calculations could be extended to determine for each recipe the number of pints you would need to drink to put you flat on your back?

CHAPTER 20

Boiling

THE sweet wort from sparging must be boiled as soon as possible after collection. Boiling marks the turning point in the process of making Beer, and must be carried out with the utmost efficiency to secure the maximum benefits.

The reasons for boiling are:—

1. Destruction of the diastase enzymes
2. Sterilisation
3. Extraction of flavour from the hops
4. Removal of haze forming matter
5. Evaporation of excess water
6. Stabilisation of salt reactions.

Even after a prolonged mash and sparging, some diastastic activity will still be present in the wort. If left unchecked, this enzyme activity could bring about a further degradation of the dextrinous sugar and could upset the delicate balance obtained so carefully during the mashing stage. The raising of the wort temperature up to boiling point completely destroys these enzymes, giving stability to the dextrin/maltose ratio and ensuring sterility of the wort.

Adding the hops

The requisite amount of hops as recommended in the recipe should be weighed on accurate kitchen scales. If they are a compressed sample, they should be broken up beforehand and inspected to ensure their freedom from any foreign matter or excessive debris. Hops can be added before boiling

157

point with the advantage that the soaking assists in reducing the tendency for the wort to "kick" in the initial stages.

The hops must always be added loose, and definitely not tied up in a muslin bag as I have often seen recommended in some recipes. The mechanical action of the hop cones passing through the boiling wort has distinct advantages, especially in the breaking of protein matter.

Some home-brewers save a proportion of the choice flavour hops and add them near the end of the boil. The reasoning behind this action is that nearly all the volatile aroma producing oils are lost in the evaporation of steam. In my point of view this is an extremely wasteful practice and is really throwing away good expensive hops. Many of the useful flavouring properties of the hop take up to an hour to be extracted and married with the malt. Leaving these additions to the last ten minutes or so, the benefits are lost, and besides, aroma can be restored more efficiently by other practices, such as dry hopping in the post fermentation period.

The first half an hour of boiling is always a difficult period. Worts will kick and bump from the boiling rolling action, and careful attention is needed to see that no spillage occurs over the side of the boiler. The scummy resinous froth from the hops builds up with alarming rapidity, and before you know where you are, the floor is covered with a sticky malt foam, generously laced with hop fragments. I doubt if there is a home-brewer of any repute in existence who has not had to hurriedly mop-up at some time or another, the wrath of his brewing boiler. Experienced hands, like myself, now regard this as part of an apprenticeship in the art of brewing!

Adding the sugar

Sugar solutions boil at a higher temperature than water. In the copper the best flavouring properties from hops are only secured at temperatures above 214°F (i.e. 2° above boiling point of water) and consequently, by adding the sugar at this stage also improves the efficiency of the boil. The sugar is dissolved in a couple of pints of the wort removed from the boiler. Pre-mixing prevents burning and caramelisation of the sugar on the boiler bottom.

158

The "hot break"

If you take a sample of the wort in a hydrometer jar and hold it up to the light it should look reasonably clear; clear, but certainly not crystal clear and bright like one would expect in the finished beer.

The change in clarity is brought about by the boiling process. A closer inspection of a light coloured wort would show that the dullness is caused by a greyish mist of finely dispersed matter. The mist is due to the presence of haze forming degraded protein matter combined with hop tannins and its derivatives.

The behaviour of these nitrogenous substances in the copper is rather remarkable. Long vigorous boils will coagulate these gummy substances and make them insoluble. Regularly observing the clarity of samples taken throughout the boil will demonstrate this fact. A few minutes after boiling commences, the mist forms a haze of small, but visible particles. The particles grow as the boiling action, coupled with the buffering of hop cones, increases the rate at which these gummy substances combine to form even larger particles.

The "hot break" is said to be secured when all the protein matter has formed into flocculating compact lumps. Always check for this condition, (but not before at least one hour's boil), by removing a wineglassful of the wort.

The thermal cycle of cooling, should, if the break is successful, deposit the match head sized particles at the bottom of the glass to leave the wort above clear of suspended matter. If there are still minute particles in suspension which have not combined with the main masses, then the wort is "undercooked" and boiling must be continued.

The wort after a good break should be very clear indeed, and with more than just a hint of sparkle. Boiling time is judged sufficient when this condition is met, but certainly not before. Longer boils may be necessary sometimes with high gravity ales, to evaporate excess water.

Thus boiling times, should, strictly speaking, never be given, and I favour the term "boil to secure the hot break". In practice, though, this condition is met by an average 1–1½ hour boil.

The wort in the boiler will look clear and black a few

minutes after the heat has been switched off, as the coagulate protein matter sinks to the bottom with the used hops. Hop seeds will float and can be skimmed off if desired.

Irish Moss

The hot break and "bright" wort can be secured better with the aid of prepared protein fining agents made from a certain type of Seaweed. Commonly known as Irish Moss or Copper Finings, these preparations are throughly recommended for all light beer production, especially high gravity ales.

The powder is mixed to a smooth paste with a little water an hour before use. It is simply added to the wort about half an hour before the turning out.

Very dark beers, especially stouts, do not need this treatment.

Hop sparge

The object of leaving the cooked wort to rest awhile is to allow the hops to sink and form a filter bed. Most of the precipitated protein matter will be retained by the spent hops when the wort is drawn off. The rate must be slow at first until the bed has formed, and then the tap can be opened as far as it is possible without affecting clarity.

Hops can absorb and retain a considerable amount of extract which must be retrieved to maintain efficiency and economy. Hop sparge with kettles of boiling water at the rate of approximately 1 pint per gallon of beer. Some of the protein matter will bound to be washed through by this action.

CHAPTER 21

Cooling

THE hot wort drawn off the boiler must be cooled as rapidly as possible for the following reasons:—

1. To bring the wort temperature down so that the yeast can be pitched before any infection sets in.
2. To achieve the "cold break".
3. To aerate the worts to assist the initial fermentation.

Wort is always better for forced cooling mainly for the reasons stated above. The sugary malt solution provides all the nutrients and creates the ideal environment for cultivating all sorts of bugs and bacteria. Once the brewers yeast has got a hold, most of these are killed off and present no problem.

A common method of forced cooling is to stand the dustbin, or polythene cube, of hot wort in a bath of cold water. Don't let it tip over. I carelessly let this happen once, and produced the best pint of Bath Salt Bitter that you have ever tasted!

Cold Break

Again, as with the Hot Break, this is a remarkable physical condition to observe. If you recall, I said that it was essential to boil the wort "bright" to a hint of sparkle to secure the Hot Break.

Now if you retain the original wineglassful of the clear hot break wort, and cool it rapidly, a most surprising phenomenon will be experienced. The wort will become cloudy again! Continue the rapid cooling and more protein matter will precipitate out of solution.

The magical appearance of cloud forming matter in what was once a clear bright wort can be most disconcerting. Again, this is protein matter formed by reaction with the tannins of malt and hops, and is more finely divided than that in the boiler. When hot it is soluble and invisible, and only makes an appearance on cooling by coagulation to larger sized particles.

Slow cooling can cause this matter to remain permanently in solution, resulting in poor clarity and fermentation. The most important consequence of a defective cold break is the imparting of an intensely harsh bitter taste to the beer. Some people attribute this taste to that very ill-defined defect of "yeast bite". It conjures up thoughts to me of little bugs jumping out from the brew in my plastic dustbin and taking a chunk out of my fingers! I must be wrong somewhere!

CHAPTER 22

Fermentation

FERMENTATION is the process by which the yeast converts the sweet wort into alcohol and carbon dioxide gas.

The most suitable container in which to conduct the primary fermentation is a plastic dustbin; the type with a twist fit lid. The dustbin should be filled by splashing the cooled wort against the inside wall to increase the amount of dissolved oxygen which is essential for yeast growth.

After checking the final volume, and topping up as necessary, the specific gravity and temperature should be checked and recorded. From the start to the finish of fermentation, the temperature should ideally be within the range 55–70°F. Practically, this can present problems, but I advise you to try to maintain the temperature as near as possible to 60°F. Fermentation will become very sluggish at temperatures below 55°F. The higher the temperature the faster becomes the yeast activity. Some people erroneously regard a faster fermentation as being best. Racing fermentations can be quite a nuisance. Attenuation is too rapid resulting in a loss of stored condition and an increased tendency for the yeast to fail to pancake in the latter stages. Fermentations conducted at temperatures exceeding 68°F have a ruinous effect on the characteristic of the yeast. The effect is similar to that experienced by plants which are force grown in greenhouses. Quick results are achieved at the expense of quality.

A yeast bred under these conditions would be a very weak strain and consequently not suitable for keeping as a pitching yeast.

A useful type of fermenter

Top fermentation

As previously stated, the action of yeast splits sugar into alcohol and CO_2 gas. The minute cells give off the gas in a very dense liquid environment. The gas, being very much lighter, rises up through the wort in the form of bubbles. Sometimes, the rising bubble takes along with it the yeast cell that initially produced the gas. On its way up to the surface it collides and combines with other like cells and forms a visible yeast projectile.

At the surface of the brew some of the bubbles burst to release the trapped gas. The remainder form a frothy mass that floats on the beer due to the buoyancy of the trapped carbon dioxide gas.

As the fermentation progresses, more and more yeast is sent up to pack on the surface until it is entirely covered with a light fluffy coating.

Until this condition is reached, the wort must be kept covered. Using a plastic dustbin, all that is needed is to replace the lid.

The low density crop should be formed within 8 hours of pitching and will become speckled with dark brown extraneous matter from hop residues, unconverted matter and "break" protein. The "boil" of fermentation tends to set up a fountain-like current that results in most of this matter being deposited as peripheral scum on the walls of the dustbin at the level of the brew. This muck should be wiped off before it hardens into a firm deposit, or alternatively mixes and ruins the flavour of the beer.

During this initial stage of fermentation, there is a marked reduction in the pH (increase in acidity) of the wort; the value dropping by about 1 unit. The extra acidity is favourable for the growth of yeast, but not for many bacteria and hence stability of the beer is improved.

After 12–24 hours the yeast crop can look quite frightening. Long meringue like tentacles of yeast reach out from the surface of the brew, some reaching 6–8 ins. in length. The contents of the dustbin look more like a "Quatermass Experiment" than beer in the making! Leave well alone. You will probably be scared to touch it anyway, and after another 8 hours the "Rocky" head, as it is called, will subside.

The surface of the crop will be quite dirty and must be skimmed. Never, though, remove the whole head of yeast. The commercial breweries can afford to skim and discard most of the crop, but this is not the case with ourselves.

Fermentation vessels in the breweries are at least twice as deep as our plastic dustbins, and therefore, for a given surface area, their systems will produce a much thicker crop of yeast. Any yeast that is skimmed off will be quickly replaced.

This is not the case with our fermentations, and we must only remove contaminated portions, so as to ensure that a protecting barrier is still maintained.

All that is needed is to pat off the oxidised scum with the back of a wooden spoon. The dirty particles readily adhere, to leave the clean crop beneath undisturbed. The second show of peripheral scum can be wiped clean at this stage as well.

The fermentation should now settle down and the yeast

crop should form a wet pancake layer approximately ¾ ins. thick over the surface of the brew.

The ability of the yeast to form the secondary pancake layer is one of the most important guides to judging and selecting a yeast for home-brewing. So many yeasts, particularly the dried granule types, are so weak that they never have the strength to form a layer. The weak strains just sink from the surface and deteriorate to produce large dirty oily bubbles which afford no protection to the beer underneath.

Sometimes the violent reaction of adding "diatomaceous earth" in the form of 1 teaspoonful of C.W.E. Wine Filtering Powder to the beer will restore the crop. Usually the head is short lived, but it is always worth trying.

Some yeasts need rousing to maintain a steady attenuation. Rousing should be carried out with a sterilised wooden spoon, the beer being "lifted" from the bottom towards the surface by a paddling action. If there is a crust on the surface, the action must be conducted so that there is minimum disturbance to the crop.

As the graphs in Appendices 1 & 2 show, after about 4 days, most of the fermentable contribution due to the sugar and maltose in the beer has been used up by the yeast. The fall in specific gravity, which has been rapid over this period, quite suddenly abates as the yeast is left with only the slow fermenting dextrinous sugars.

The change point is quoted as a fraction of original gravity. For normal top fermenting brew made with the infusion mash system, it is known as the "Quarter Gravity" stage resulting from the fact that the wort will contain approximately 25 per cent of dextrinous sugars.

The subsequent fall in specific gravity will be very much slower and thus the beer now enters what is called the "secondary fermentation" period.

Secondary fermentation

The yeast crop at the end of the primary fermentation should be skimmed off and discarded. Check and record the specific gravity at this stage.

The beer can no longer by left in the dustbin exposed and open to all sorts of airborne infections. Vessels are needed in which the beer can be stored with the exclusion of air.

166

Gallon jars with airlocks or polythene cubes make ideal recipients for the green beer. They should be cleaned and sterilised before use.

The gallon jars should be filled to within $\frac{1}{2}$ in. of the underside of the airlock bung, which incidentally, must be made of rubber. The traps in the airlocks should preferably be filled with glycerine. If a polythene cube is being used then the tap can be removed and the airlock bung will fit nicely into the bore that is left.

About half way through racking, transfer the syphon tube and fill up a wine bottle to the base of the neck with beer. Fold a small square of polythene sheet over the neck and secure with an elastic band. This pilot bottle gives a quick visual indication of the clarification and progress of the main brew.

The secondary fermentation allows the beer to settle and partially clarify under sterile conditions. If needed, the beer can be left for a month in these conditions without further attention.

Bottom fermentation

Bottom fermenting yeasts are excellent for home-brewing and are far superior to the top fermenting varieties for bottle and barrel conditioning. By working from the bottom of the vessel in later processes, clearer, brighter beers can be produced.

Lager yeasts, as they are often called, are derived from pure strains of yeast and tend to be a far more stable product. Continental practice favours conducting the fermentation at much lower temperatures than would be experienced in our English systems. Primary fermentation is carried out between 40 and 50°F, followed by a prolonged secondary fermentation a few degrees above freezing point. The physical and practical parameters imposed by these systems put them out of the scope of most home-brewers.

The yeast, however, can be used with considerable advantage with infusion mash worts fermented under English practice.

Yeast crops are still experienced on the surface of the brew, but not in such a spectacular manner as the top fermenting varieties. Management of the fermentation is also similar. Extra care is needed with the removal of unwanted matter from the surface of the brew, since the crop, and all the impurities that it contains, will sink back into the wort at the end of the primary fermentation.

The beer can lose its protective head of yeast within a matter of a couple of hours after fermentation abates, hence it is advisable to err on the safe side and rack off into closed containers before the quarter gravity stage is reached. Do not get misled over the racking gravity with bottom fermenting yeasts. The racking gravity is solely a function of maltose/dextrin ratio of the wort and not dependent on the type of yeast.

The "third gravity" stage racking of continental lagers is because the wort contains a third dextrinous sugar. It would still have to be racked at this stage even if it was pitched with a top fermenting ale yeast.

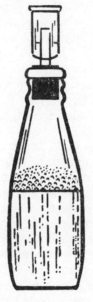

Yeast Starter Bottle

CHAPTER 23

Finings

FINING is the method of clarifying beer by the removal of suspended yeast using prepared additives to accelerate the natural processes.

The major cause of beer going "off" during storage is due to the presence of yeast. Home brewed beer must for economic reasons be naturally conditioned and thus this problem is of particular interest to us. Yeast, being a living organism, will inevitably deteriorate with age, and the decomposition of the dead cells will eventually impart an objectionable taint to the beer. The degree of effect and the length of storage is dependent largely on the amount, type and condition of the yeast present.

Yeast must obviously be present to provide gas conditioning through the breakdown of the residual fermentable carbohydrates that are left in the beer for this purpose. Technically then, it is better to leave just the absolute minimum amount of yeast that will ensure efficient carbonation. In practice, the most consistent method to achieve this aim is to remove all the yeast from the beer, and then add a minute amount which practice has proved sufficient to maintain conditioning.

The best time to use finings is a couple of days before bottling or casking. For normal recommended fermentation practice, this would be after the beer has rested for about

5 days in the secondary fermentation vessel. The gravity of bottled beer must be allowed to stabilise first, so that an accurate assessment can be made of the fermentable sugars that could still produce troublesome condition. Bottled beer then must be allowed to work out in the secondary fermentation. Five days with no fall in specific gravity is acceptable proof of this condition, even although the reading may still give an S.G. 8–12.

Beer for casking in pressure barrels with safety vents can be fined after a day or two of secondary settling.

The stage of secondary fermentation and the subsequent treatment of the beer has a direct influence on the selection of the fining agent. Two types are available, both chemically related and are glutinous animal products.

1. Gelatine
2. Isinglass

Gelatine

Gelatine is the best and most convenient form of fining available to the Home-brewer. Not all types and grades are suitable, but the one I use for the majority of my brews is the common household Gelatine. Sold in nearly every grocery store that I have been in, under the name of "Davis's Gelatine", it is supplied in a carton containing five sachets. Each sachet is capable of fining a five gallon brew of beer starbright in less than 24 hours.

The contents of the sachet are made up by a preliminary mixing of the dry granules with a few tablespoons of cold water to form a smooth paste, and then diluting further with half a pint of cold water. The solution requires gentle heat to dissolve the gelatine completely. Warm the saucepan over a low heat, stirring continuously until the contents dissolve clear. DO NOT BOIL, as this will degrade the gelatine and impair its fining action. The finings must be thoroughly mixed with the beer before it cools and solidifies. The hot liquid is such a small bulk compared with the main brew that no thermal problems should be experienced. Stir and agitate for 2 or 3 minutes to ensure a consistent dispersion and then leave the beer to settle. A "squirt" of stock Sodium Met., from Squeezy dispenser in the brew will also help the fining.

170

The fining action of Gelatine is purely mechanical. For our small brews where the object is to completely purge the beer of suspended matter, this fining agent is ideal, but for larger commercial ventures it would prove uneconomic.

Isinglass

Isinglass is the swimming bladder of the Sturgeon. How on earth it was found to be a means of clearing beer I will never comprehend! I must admit that the thought of having the shredded stomach of a fish floating about in my beer did not enamour my feelings towards this fining agent. Later I found out that Gelatine was made from Calves Heels, so I felt that I was no better off with its alternative!

It has the advantage over Gelatine in that its fining action is mainly by the neutralisation of the electrical charge of the yeast rather than by mechanical means. Practically, less Isinglass is needed than Gelatine for the same degree of fining but, the big disadvantage with Isinglass is that it is difficult to prepare and difficult to store when prepared.

Dried Isinglass will keep indefinitely. To be made up into a fining agent it must be dissolved in a dilute acid solution. This "cutting" process can take days with a high quality sample to render it into a glutinous mass suitable for fining purposes. Once it has been made up it must be kept cool. Temperatures not much above 70°F can cause it to go "slack" and be useless for finings.

If you can ensure that the temperature of the beer can be kept reasonably cool (below 65°F) then these finings are ideal, and even better than Gelatine, for pressure barrel fining.

On the market now there are commercially prepared Isinglass solutions with a better thermal stability. Coupled with these are Auxiliary Finings, a preparation added a few hours before the main finings, to accelerate the action of the isinglass. A brighter brew is thus obtained more quickly.

Isinglass preparations are not recommended for clearing bottom fermenting yeasts. The electrical charge, or something just as silly, is wrong which prevents an efficient action. Either gelatine, or alternatively, hazel wood chips must be used. The latter fining agent should test your ingenuity and enthusiasm for being a keen beermaker!

171

Final adjustments

At the same time as finings are added, other minor adjustments can be made to alter the character of the beer.

The hop flavour and aroma can be increased and enhanced by small requisite doses of proprietary hop oils. In the absence of some commercial preparation, the bitterness can be increased by using "Hop Tea". Take an ounce or so of choice hops, place them in a saucepan and pour over them just sufficient boiling water to cover them completely. After a few minutes strain off the "tea" and add this to the main brew. The actual amount to be added must be judged by taste.

Heading liquids, if deemed necessary, can also be added at this stage. Remember that bottled beer can only tolerate about a third of the dose for draught beers.

Final colouring and tinting can be done by cautiously added caramel solutions to the brew. Be extremely wary and always err on the light side when making colour adjustments at this stage. The suspended yeast can give a completely false indication of the colour of the beer. Colouring is really best carried out in the boiler, and final tinting *after* fining. Caramel not boiled into solution may not be completely stable throughout maturation.

Filtering

Filtering, as yet, is not a very successful method of clearing beer in home-brewing. The beer has to be filtered within a totally enclosed circuit to exclude air and the risk of infection and oxidisation.

The wine filters that are on the market are generally not man enough to cope with the quantity of yeast in beer.

There is a real need on the home-brew market for a good system of filtering beer.

CHAPTER 24

Bottled beer

BOTTLING beer is a convenient means of reducing the brew into more manageable quantities. Manageable quantities in handling, not in thirst, I hasten to add!

All home-brewed beer must in essence be naturally conditioned, and it is this type of beer that has always been reckoned to possess the finest flavour. Conditioning in the bottle implies that secondary fermentation will continue due to the action of yeast on the residual sugar in the beer, formed naturally or by added primings. The gas liberated by this action is trapped within the bottle and is dissolved in the beer.

When the bottle is opened after a suitably long maturation and poured, the release of gas brings sparkle and zest to the drink and that desirable briskness to the palate as well as promoting a pleasing frothy head over the surface.

Bottling Gravity

Grain beers do not ferment out to zero gravity. For bottling purposes, they can be considered to have stopped

173

working at a specific gravity between 8 and 12. This desirable characteristic gives these quality beers the body and fullness of palate so lacking in other types of home-made beers.

The particular point where the beer stops working cannot be predetermined, and hence bottling must not be gauged to a set figure of specific gravity.

The carbohydrates in beer can be classified by the degree of fermentability. Primary fermentation is vigorous because of the readily fermentable household sugars and the maltose derived from the grain. Once these sugars have been used up, the rate of attenuation slows down as the yeast is left with the less fermentable dextrins. The transition from primary to secondary fermentation is positively identifiable by the vigour of yeast activity.

It is the progress and performance of the yeast after the "quarter" gravity stage has been reached that is not quite so definite. These dextrinous sugars can be broadly classified as "slowly fermentable" and "unfermentable".

The slowly fermentable sugars roughly constitute 5 per cent of the starting gravity. For instance, as shown in the specimen fermentation appendices, the beer with a starting gravity of 50 has a quarter gravity stage, by definition, of S.G. 12·5. The remaining 2·5° drop in gravity takes another 4 days or so to reach its final gravity of 10. The latter drop is due to the slow fermenting "conditioning" dextrinous sugars. The rest of the carbohydrates that fill the final gravity section are not totally unfermentable as stated, but will, over a few months, bring about a further drop of 1–2 degrees. Account must be taken of this phenomenon when bottling high gravity long maturing ales.

The recommended procedure for bottling is to allow the beer to use up the "conditioning" sugar so that stability can be assured. Five days with no fall in specific gravity is my personal judgement on this matter.

Bottles

Only use beer bottles.

Bottled beer is a pressurised system and must be treated with the respect it deserves. Commercial beer bottles are easily obtainable and are custom built to withstand the internal gas pressure that builds up inside. Cracked or chipped

174

bottles must not be used, as their mechanical strength is impaired.

The common sizes are the quart, pint, half pint and the nip (third pint). Gradually, though, these are being phased out of use as the metric quarter, third, half, and one litre sizes come into favour. Beer bottles are still usually dark coloured, a left over tradition from when all bottled beer was naturally conditioned. The brown or green colours enhanced the looks of the product by obscuring the yeast deposit and also protected the beer from the actinic effect of light. The old style screw stopper closures are also being replaced by the more modern metal crown caps or plastic reseals.

Preparing the bottles

The bottles must be washed and cleaned with plain hot water (no detergents, please!). Make absolutely certain that every deposit or trace of contamination is removed from the bottle. My custom built bottle brush and the procedure for "seeing in the dark" make short work of the task.

Bottle washing is an ideal punishment for naughty and disobedient kids, as well as poor unsuspecting Cub Scouts on Job Week. I think my house has been "blacked" by the atter organisation!

To prove the worth of cleanness in the bottle, try the following practical test. Select one of your bottles with a deposit of old yeast; scrape out a minute quantity and taste it. I am pretty certain that you will increase your standards of cleaning after this test! The taste, besides being revolting, is instantly recognisable as the common "off flavour" found in far too many home-brewed beers.

The bottles can be sterilised after cleaning using 2 tablespoonsful of standard stock solution diluted in about half a pint of hot water. Line up the bottles, and pour the solution from one bottle to another using a funnel. Each bottle must be adequately swilled with the solution and then upturned to drain. So long as the bottles are drained fairly well, the dregs of sterilising solution can remain inside. Each bottle should be primed with a scant half teaspoonful of white sugar per pint to promote secondary conditioning. The stoppers can be loosely replaced to keep the bottles sweet.

Preparing the beer

The beer for bottling must be star bright and crystal clear. Cloudy beer will not keep. Excessive deposits of yeast will also cause clouding of the beer when the bottle is opened, ruining the flavour and making the drink look unattractive. After the secondary fermentation conditioning; beer for bottling must be fined. As well as ensuring clarity, it will remove the majority of the stale primary yeast. Top fermenting yeast should generally be removed from all bottled beers, since their characteristics and keeping qualities are not conducive to the long storage times.

The beer should be racked quietly off the fined debris into another closed container, such as a pressure barrel or polythene cube.

Half to three quarters of a teaspoonful of bottom ferfermenting Lager yeast granules should be creamed with a little sugar and water to form a smooth solution, and then be added to the clear beer. The "krausen" yeast as it is called, must be thoroughly dispersed in the clear beer, by rolling or rocking the container. "Mad" condition is released from the beer by this action which must be vented carefully, otherwise you may have the doubtful privilege of launching the first orbiting batch of beer!

The beer bottles can now be filled by siphoning from the main container. The flow of the beer can be controlled by squeezing the rubber tube of the bottle filling end, and the rate of filling is governed by the difference in levels of bottles and the filling container. A large difference in levels will result in a fast flow. Each bottle should be filled to within ¾ in. of the underside of the stopper. After filling, the stopper should be loosely placed in position whilst the siphon tube is transferred to the next bottle for filling. This sequence is maintained until all the bottles are filled.

Not securing the stoppers immediately has the advantage that the bottling reaction will drive off any air above the surface of the beer, thus reducing oxidisation and expelling any bacteria.

Screw stoppers and plastic reseals should be fixed as applicable, and the bottles shaken to dissolve the sugar and the outside surface wiped clean of spilt beer.

176

Siphoning into bottles

Crown Caps must be applied using the lever operated device of the Crown Capper, a female punch that needs to be hammered to impress the metal caps on to the bottles.

Screw stopper .... and crown cork

Priming with sugar

Labelling

Every beer bottle looks alike, and it is virtually impossible to identify the contents by outward appearances. In wine you can have crafty "sippers" without affecting the contents too much, but the nature of beer will not permit such an approach. No matter how much you try to convince yourself, you can never identify with full confidence, the contents of two or three brews bottled at the same time in unmarked bottles.

Always label every bottle.

The most convenient method I have found is by using the packs of small, circular, self adhesive labels. Each pack of 700, 8 mm. labels, costs only a few pence, and contains four or five different colours. My bottling code is:—

Red	—	Bitter
Yellow	—	Lager
Blue	—	Stouts
White	—	Pales and Lights
Green	—	Browns

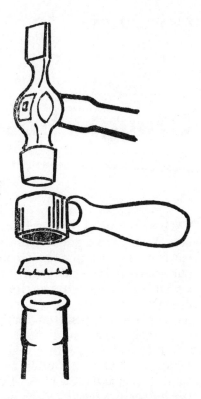

Applying crown corks with a simple tool and hammer. Lever corking tools are even better, but slightly dearer

Labels can be further identified numbering the batch Thus, the yellow disc with 7 on it would be a bottle of my seventh brew of Lager. A similar numbered disc is stuck in my recipe book as a quick reference. The system can be extended to cover experimental brews and even the same brew, where individual gallons were subjected to different treatment.

Storing

Bottles must be stored in an upright position in a cool dark place. The temperature of storage has a considerable influence on the quality of the beer.

The object is ideally to keep the bottle at the lower temperature at which the yeast can work to provide condition.

CHAPTER 25

Draught beer

THE majority of beer drinkers prefer draught to bottled beer. I am no exception, and thus I have been rather frustrated over the fact that the amateur trade failed to recognise our needs, and has taken them 10 years or more to supply us with a really reliable system for dispensing our home brew on draught. Nowadays though, it is possible to purchase equipment that will dispense efficiently, 4 pints to 5 gallons of beer on draught, so all is forgiven!

Life had been rather difficult and inconvenient before. I had to swallow my pride and go down to the local if I wanted to enjoy a few pints of draught. Taking one back for the missus was awkward as well. A thirty-six gallon barrel of draught stout is very heavy and difficult to steer on the pavement after you have had a few pints. Barrels are such a stupid shape. Being bulbous in the middle, one kick slightly off centre will cause the barrel to gyrate across the road at an alarming speed. Although retrieving it becomes tiresome, it is a wonderful experience to watch the reflexes of passing motorists. Those were the days!

Stout, bitter, and mild ale are the best beers for draught production. The techniques and management of the beer require some subtle differences in approach to that of bottled beer. Mainly it is the conditioning aspects that pose the differences.

Draught beer requires a higher proportion of the slow fermenting dextrinous sugars to produce the essential cask conditioning. Conducting the mashing stage at temperatures slightly above 150°F with stiff mashes can be conducive to producing these sugars. Fermenting at lower temperature will also help by increasing the solubility, and hence the amount, of conditioning gas that can be dissolved into the beer.

Malt conditioning, as distinct from primings, is a far more satisfactory means of carbonating the bulk, and this in turn can be generally best controlled through the use of finings. Practically, this method of controlled fining suits our home brewed beer very well.

The object of controlled fining technique is to clear the beer of yeast a few degrees above the quarter gravity stage. Attenuation should just be starting to slow down to the point where finings can be added without causing too many problems. If the gravity is too high, the yeast activity and the evolution of gas will give buoyancy to the finings, preventing the "drop out". The temperature of the beer is an important consideration. If the beer can be chilled (to about 50°F) by transferring it to a cold place, then fining and clarification is likely to be more successful.

The treatment must be started in the dustbin stage at the latter end of the primary fermentation. Select the racking gravity by adding 2 or 3 degrees to the quarter gravity figure. For example, a beer with a starting gravity of 40 should be racked off at (40 divided by 4 plus 2) which gives a S.G. of 12.

Rack the beer off gently into another sterilised container equal to the capacity of the brew. Large pressure barrels of "ex. wine" polythene cubes are ideal for five gallon batches. Near the end of racking, siphon off a sample of the beer into a large sized clear wine bottle. Fill the bottle leaving 1½ ins. of air space, and place over the neck a small square of polythene sheet secured in position with an elastic band. Store the sample in the refrigerator or another cool place.

Add finings to the main bulk and shake well to ensure an adequate dispersion. Vent the "mad" condition and draw off another sample, which this time contains finings, and siphon into a wine bottle and seal as before. This latter sample and the main bulk can then be transferred to a cool place for clarification to take place.

Within an hour, the fined sample should show positive signs of clearing. After a day or so, it should be absolutely starbright. The pilot sample of fined beer gives the indication of when the main brew will be ready, and also a preview of the finished beer. By sampling the clear beer at the top of the bottle through a drinking straw, the taste and flavour can be assessed and a decision made as to the need for minor adjustment to the main brew.

Colour, hop bitterness, and sweetness can all be increased if deemed necessary. The main bulk of the brew must be racked off the fined debris before any adjustments are made. Racking can usually be carried out into its final dispensers.

The clear beer should be "krausened" with the yeast-saturated sample taken from the first racking.

Containers and dispensers for draught beer

Draught beer is the most convenient means of dispensing our brews. Bottle washing can become a tedious chore and sometimes cleaning a beer bottle can take longer than it takes to drink the beer inside! With just one container to clean and sterilise, barrels are a popular choice on the grounds of convenience.

Plastic pressure barrels

Plastic pressure barrels, like the one shown on page 29 were the first custom built containers for the amateur trade for dispensing beer on draught. Being prototypes, many of these containers experienced serious teething troubles. Inefficient seals and leaky taps were the main problems which left many home brewers disillusioned and disappointed with the arrangement.

The latest barrels have been extensively redesigned with many improved features, and are now probably the most thoroughly proven and tested system available to the home brewer and are guaranteed to give many years satisfactory service.

The barrels, which come in 5¼ and 2¼ gallon sizes, are made of rigid plastic and are designed to free stand vertically. There is a well below the tap level to retain the yeast deposited by the secondary fermentation. The filler cap at the top is designed to take a plain sealing cap, or the cap plus an injector unit.

182

Operating conditions

It is interesting to delve into the theory of home brewed draught beer, and the design of these barrels to show how they can be used to the utmost advantage.

The barrels are made of high density plastic to give adequate mechanical strength, pleasing appearance and easy maintenance. Plastic, although light and convenient, cannot obviously be expected to withstand the same pressures as the like sized metal kegs used by the commerical trade. The limit for these barrels is 10 p.s.i., which is a perfectly adequate pressure for dispensing draught beer.

When pulling a pint of draught beer, it is desirable that the dispensing pressure remains sensibly constant. The consistency of dispensing pressure with a self contained unit, is largely dependent on the gas space above the beer. And the larger the gas space, the more even is the gas pressure.

In a 5 gallon barrel with 1 gallon of gas volume above the beer, a gallon of beer could be drawn off before the pressure is lost. But, if the volume was only 1 pint above the beer, then only half a pint of beer could be drawn off before all the pressure was lost. These are the laws of nature, and thus cannot be overcome. The pressure will always partially restore as the conditioning gas comes out of solution to restore the balance: the actual amount depending on how much gas was originally in solution in the beer, and the temperature.

It is rather a frustrating experience having a barrel filled with five gallons of good beer, and only being able to pull off half a pint or so every hour. Releasing the cap to restore atmospheric pressure would do the trick, but it would also draw in air that would make the beer go "off" in a very short space of time. Leaving the tap open and allowing the air to bubble back through the beer would also restore the pressure, but again it would invite the same trouble. The beer would only dribble out under these circumstances to make it a very unattractive drink.

Adding extra priming sugar to produce more gas is not the answer as the safe working pressure of the barrel may be exceeded.

To maintain a steady ejection pressure and complete sterility of the brew, these plastic pressure barrels must be fitted with a carbon dioxide gas injector unit. These devices,

183

which fit on the cap as an integral unit, provide a protective blanket of CO_2 gas over the surface of the brew giving head pressure as well as ensuring a sterile environment; a condition much needed when the natural gas in the barrel is spent.

The carbon dioxide gas, which is the same as that given off during fermentation, is supplied from small pressurised gas cartridges called "Sparklet bulbs". The replaceable bulbs are held within the hollow handle and are screwed into the unit to form an airtight seal before the cartridge is punctured to release the gas. Another feature is that the unit incorporates a safety valve set as 10 p.s.i.; the safe working pressure of the barrels.

The safety valve has an important secondary role in that it permits far more scope for conditioning the beer. The more conditioning gas that can be coaxed into solution, the better these barrels will work. Hence the more gas that is passed through the beer, the more chance there is of it being dissolved. Condition is more readily absorbed this way than by relying on the thermal currents to carry the head pressure into solution.

The extra gas can be provided simply by increasing the dose of priming sugar. The only limiting factors on the amount of sugar are the time that it takes for the beer to clear after this activity, and also the increase in alcoholic content of the beer may be regarded as undesirable.

Excessive gas pressure generated by the sugar is vented off by the safety valve.

More weight of gas can be contained in a given volume of air space than in the equivalent volume of beer. For small volumes, the gas pressure will quickly rise and be vented off. Larger air spaces provide a greater cushioning effect for more weight of gas to be stored before the venting pressure is exceeded. Thus larger air spaces above the beer give a better store of natural condition. The theory is opposite to what is really wanted. The barrel wants to be filled with beer, not gas! Obviously a compromise has to be made between the loss of beer space and the loss of conditioning gas.

From my experience, a large pressure barrel should be filled with $4\frac{1}{4}$ gallons of beer so as to leave 1 gallon of air space for natural conditioning pressure. Similarly, the smaller barrels should be filled with $1\frac{3}{4}$ gallons of beer to leave $\frac{1}{2}$ a gallon of space.

Leaving such an air space is an open invitation for infection. Fortunately, the way over this problem is simple. After filling the barrel with beer add three teaspoonsful of stock sterilising solution and replace the injector unit. Gently crack open the control valve of the injector and allow the gas pressure to build up until the rubber on the safety valve lifts. Let the barrel and its contents stand quiet for a few minutes, and then twist to crack the seal of the filler cap to release a gush of gas. Reseal the cap. The carbon dioxide gas injected from the unit is heavier than air, so that after a few minutes rest it will sink and form a layer beneath the air. Releasing the cap will cause the lighter layer of air to be expelled. Open the control valve again to allow more CO_2 gas into the barrel until the safety valve blows for about 1 second. The second purge of gas should ensure that any remaining air will be expelled so that the beer can now condition under a sterile gas blanket. The dose of Sodium Metabisulphite will take care of any "bugs" that escaped the first treatment.

So long as the beer can be fully charged with natural conditioning then the barrel will provide some first class draught beer. Two or three of the 4 gramme Sparklet Bulbs will still be necessary to eject all the beer from a large barrel, and 1 or 2 for the smaller size. Bigger gas bulbs (12 gramme) are now available and will cut down the cartridge replacement proportionately.

Priming sugar must, however, still be added to the barrels. As stated above, the priming rate can be rather excessive so long as the filler cap incorporates a safety valve. 4 ozs. of white sugar will prime the larger barrel, and 2 ozs. the smaller one.

The activity set up by the addition of primings will take a week or two to abate. Special fining mixture (Auxiliary plus isinglass) especially designed for use with these barrels should be used to aid reclarification.

The Homebrews and Brew-it-Yourself Brukegs are excellent types of these barrels that have been proved to withstand the test of time, and all the physical abuse that home brewers can muster.

185

Eurokegs

Eurokegs are an efficient means of handling small quantities of home brewed draught beer. The simplicity and convenience of these kegs has made the system a firm favourite of mine. Basically, the system uses one injector unit together with a number of individually sealed P.V.C. pressure vessels. The P.V.C. "pods" are ball shaped, with a rimmed flat bottom and come in 10 pint and 7 pint capacities.

Four large or six small pods will split up a 5 gallon brew into convenient units. Each pod can then be filled and sealed with a plain cap (injector is not necessary at this stage). The containers can then be stored away to condition and mature, and can even be shelved in a similar manner to the winemaker with his gallon jars. Incidentally, Eurokegs are the nearest thing for producing an instant sparkling wine!

By careful management of the beer in ensuring cool or chilled conditions during secondary fermentation and racking, there is often sufficient CO_2 absorbed in the beer for it to be casked in these pods without priming for additional conditioning. Starbright "keg" clarity can be achieved, and the injector unit needs only to provide the ejection gas. The pods are small enough to allow this approach to be adopted. Gas is cheaper to produce from sugar than from Sparklets Bulbs, so I usually prefer to adopt natural conditioning.

Yeast clouding is minimal with these units and rarely causes any embarrassment.

The high priming rate recommended for the plastic pressure barrels must not be apportioned down to suit these units, since they do not possess an automatic pressure relief device. Priming rates of half a teaspoonful per pint of capacity should not be exceeded.

The dispenser unit is an integral pressure supplying and maintaining device, coupled with the tap and "pull" handle. One pays for these extra features, but I consider that the investment is well worthwhile.

The great advantage with these dispensers over some other types is the pressure maintaining feature. Ejection pressure is kept constant automatically and therefore eliminates the need to operate a control valve to balance the outflow from the tap. If there is insufficient condition in the beer, the action of pulling the handle forwards operates a valve to

186

draw extra gas from the CO_2 bulb. The unit is designed to use all the natural condition first thereby usefully discriminating on the grounds of economy. Another advantage is that the tap outlet is sufficiently far from the base to permit a glass to be filled without first positioning the pod on a shelf.

The dispenser unit is fitted to the pod by spiking the rubber insert with the projecting stainless steel draw off tube. The pod reseals as the unit is push-clamped on to the top and depresses the rubber insert.

The beer can be drawn off immediately by placing a glass beneath the tap and pulling the handle forward.

Sparklets beertap

Another type of integral tap and dispenser unit is the Sparklets Beertap. The units do a grand job, and are well made and designed, but being constructed mainly from plastic they are not quite so robust as the Eurokeg system. At a couple of pounds cheaper, who can complain?

Two types are available for using with the conventional pressure barrels or the metal "pipkins".

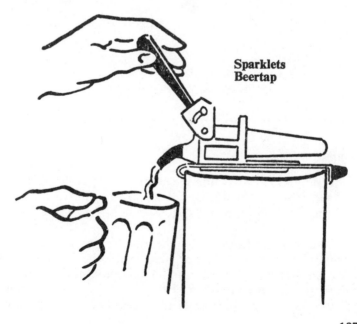

Sparklets
Beertap

187

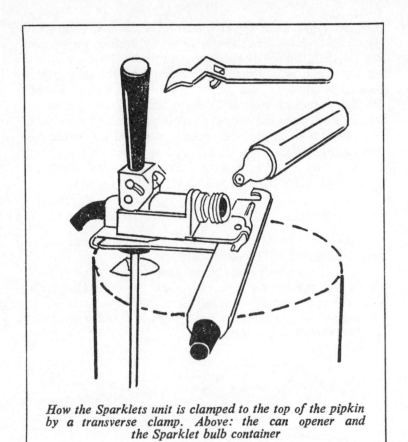

How the Sparklets unit is clamped to the top of the pipkin by a transverse clamp. Above: the can opener and the Sparklet bulb container

Pipkins

The pipkin injector unit is designed to fit both the 4 pint or 7 pint standard sized cans. Beer can be drawn off right down to the last few ounces; the last pint being as clear as the first.

Similar procedures as for the Eurokeg pods should be adopted for these cans. After filling with the beer, a solid rubber grommet is plugged into the filler hole, and the pipkin can be stored away in a cool place to mature and condition. All one has to do when the can is required, is to remove the plug (chill the can first if possible) and push fit on the beertap and clamp it into position.

A thick rubber washer on the underside of the tap seals the can to the unit. Hey Presto!, beer is there just for the want of pulling.

Pressure barrel beertap

The Sparklets Beertap combined with the plastic pressure barrels are the ultimate in convenience, economy, and effort for dealing with the larger quantities of home brew. The sparklet unit screws on to the filler cap thread and its design solves the two major problems with the straight barrel/injector system. The plastic barrels have the draw off tap at the bottom, which means that the cask must be positioned on a shelf or similar place so as to provide enough room beneath the tap for filling the glass. A full barrel can weigh the best part of a half hundredweight, so it can be a bit of a struggle for your wife when you send her off to pull you a pint!

Also, the regulation of pressure must be done manually by operating the control valve, which can be very wasteful on CO_2 gas if the exercise is not conducted with the utmost delicacy.

The Sparklets Beertap has the tap at the top and will also tend to regulate the ejection pressure. The barrel can therefore remain on the floor, and pint after pint can be pulled off with no trouble at all, except for the occasional change of gas cartridge.

Sparklets automatic pressure injector

The problem of having to operate manually the control valve on the standard CO_2 injector for plastic pressure barrels has now been overcome. The function of the control valve has now been made completely automatic in the Sparklets automatic injector unit. Gas pressure is constantly regulated to about 12 p.s.i.

Other Systems

Many other systems and products are available on the home brew market for dispensing beer, but it would be impracticable for me to discuss them all. I have not tried and tested them all, so consequently I am not really in a position to comment. Generally, you get what you pay for, and I feel sure that there are other methods of dispensing beer that are equally as good as the types covered above. From my comments on the various systems and the theory of operation, I hope you can find some guidance to assist you in purchasing one of these other systems if you feel that it will suit your set-up better.

CHAPTER 26

Beer from the wood

THE traditional method of drawing beer from wooden casks is rapidly disappearing in the commercial field due to economic pressures. Unfortunately, wooden casks do not lend themselves to modern production techniques, nor do they bring out the best in the low gravity ales of today. Breweries protest that the taxation prevents them from turning out a high gravity beer that would do justice in these wooden casks. Consequently, the few remaining casks are filled with standard brews that were specifically designed for the metal keg containers and not wooden barrels.

Most of the brews that I have tasted lately "from the wood" have been, quite frankly, disappointing. They are inferior in flavour, clarity, and head retention to those served from modern casks. We have now reached such a degree of competence in our craft, that we can easily take over where the commercial breweries have left off and produce our own finest quality beer drawn from the wood.

The most convenient cask sizes for our brews are the keg (6 gallons), and the pin (4½ gallons). As breweries phase these casks out of production, it can be quite easy to pick one up in good condition for a small sum. The cask must be perfectly intact and completely free from mechanical damage.

Reconditioning a cask

One of the major problems with casks for breweries is the high cost of maintenance. Wood, being porous, is very susceptible to infection. The rough internal surfaces tend to collect and retain deposits to provide an ideal breeding ground for bacteria. Thorough cleaning and sterilisation is obviously very important.

Casks of unknown origin or that have a doubtful history should undergo a full reconditioning procedure.

The tap and bung should be removed, and the peg hole in the flat wooden shive blocked with a cut off hard peg. The tap aperture needs to be bunged with a tapered cork. Corks that fit 1 gallon jars are ideal for this purpose. Dissolve in hot water, 2 heaped tablespoonsful of Silana P.F. crystals for every gallon of capacity of the casks. Funnel this solution through the small bung hole, and then fill the cask with very hot water. Replace the filler bung and roll the cask for a few minutes to disperse the solution.

Roll the cask 2 or 3 times daily for the next 3 days. After rolling the cask up and down the lawn a couple of times you begin to feel like a chimpanzee in the zoo performing his party tricks; but never mind, it's all in a good cause!

Drain and hose out the contents after the 3 days, and refill the cask with hot water and 2 ounces of sodium Metabisulphite powder. Repeat the rolling procedure and clean out again after another 2 days.

To make absolutely sure that the cask is free from taints, I recommend carrying out a short fermentation inside it. Add 2 pounds of sugar as a syrup, a tablespoonful of nutrient or malt extract, and half an ounce of beer yeast to the barrel and fill up with cool water to the bung hole. Temporarily replace the bung and roll the cask to mix the ingredients. Take out the bung and leave the cask in a warm place. Stand the cask on a large tray to catch the yeast that frets from the small bung hole.

After 4 or 5 day's fermentation discard the contents and wash out the cask and sterilise with normal strength stock solution before finally rinsing.

Remove the tap bung and check that the bore is smooth and clean. Tap in a new dry wooden tap with a mallet. Replace the shive, hard peg, and bung with new ones as necessary.

The stillage for the barrel can be cut and shaped from any hard wood whilst the barrel is undergoing its reconditioning.

192

Beer for the wood

The beer intended for operating on the wood must preferably be of high gravity, and must also contain a high proportion of the slow fermenting dextrinous sugars. Starting gravities between 50 and 60° are ideal, especially if the goods are mashed between 150 and 154°F.

A barrel like this stands on robust 'stillage," and is closed by a "shive" which houses the "peg" used for admitting air as necessary. Beer is drawn-off through the bottom tap.

The temperature of fermentation and racking must be kept as low as possible and certainly not allowed to rise above 65°F. The ejection and condition of the beer relies entirely on the gas produced by secondary fermentation, which in turn is dependent on the temperature at which the various processes were conducted. We cannot stick on an injector unit into a wooden barrel!

The fermentation, racking, and storage are best carried out in a cool "cellar" such as a garage or outhouse. "Cutting" the fermentation just before the quarter gravity stage using the controlled fining technique, is a useful means of ensuring adequate condition. The beer must always be fined crystal clear before it is racked into the barrel. Again, to preserve the primary condition, racking must be done as slowly and as quietly as possible. Finings and primings, and the yeast-saturated wine bottle sample should be added to the beer.

On the stillage, the small bung should be hammered home, and the flat shive at the top removed to facilitate filling. The cask should be filled to capacity. Lay a sterilised wine filtering bag, folded double, or a clean coarse rag over the metal bush surrounding the shive hole, and mallet in a shive shaped cork. This arrangement gives the right degree of porosity to vent the excess gas during the initial, lively cask conditioning.

A new shive should be prepared by removing the peg shaped centre. Nowadays, these are usually the partially cut "knock-out" type. When the cask condition quietens down to a continuous, but very slight hiss, the bag and bung can be removed. Now is the best time to add dry hops. A small handful of high grade hops, such as East Kent Goldings, will do much to restore the lost aroma and will enhance the character and quality of the beer. Dry hops must remain in the cask for at least 3 weeks to achieve the maximum benefit from their flavouring properties.

Hammer in the hard wood shive and block the vent in it with a soft wood peg. Slackening the peg gives a finer control of conditioning. After a week or so when the escaping gas is hardly audible, the soft peg can be replaced with a hard one.

With the hard peg in a gas tight position, draw off some of the beer from the tap. If a pint or so can be drawn off by the action of the pressure in the barrel, so much the better.

The space above the beer (called ullage), will act as a cushion and store for the subsequent condition that is given off.

Allow another week to pass before tapping the barrel. The beer should be brisk and lively, and many pints should be able to be drawn off under its own "steam". Do not, however, flog the barrel and try to draw off more beer than will pressure off naturally. It is far better to wait a day or so for the condition to build up again, rather than risk the remainder going off through drawn-in air.

194

After a couple of gallons have been drawn off, the barrel will need repriming. Make up a sugar solution on the basis of half an ounce per gallon of beer left in the barrel. Remove the hard peg and funnel the solution into the barrel. Replace the hard peg, and shake the barrel to effect dispersion, and leave it to condition for another week before sampling.

The remaining beer can usually be easily drawn off after these secondary primings have worked out.

It is a great thrill to draw your own beer from the wood. The management of this beer is an art, and it may take years to develop all the skills. I am by no means an expert, but I take comfort in the fact that I am learning the art of one of our most treasured crafts, and that perhaps my efforts will prolong the traditions of our heritage.

CHAPTER 27

Maturation

MATURATION is the aging process that allows the beer to develop character under sterile conditions.

A mature beer implies that it is in the peak of condition, and possesses stability, fullness of flavour, a fine bead and bouquet, together with a soft round palate with a pleasing head and general appearance. Naturally conditioned beers can only be brought to this perfection through time. The personality of the beer must develop over a period and be moulded by the correct environment to achieve these attributes.

Well-made beer can be ruined by bad maturation, and thus it would be foolish not to abide by a few simple rules to ensure that the beer develops to the best of its ability.

The production of conditioning gas within the bottle will inherently bring problems regarding clarity, consistent carbonation, and shelf life. Careful management and common sense at bottling time will do much to minimise these problems.

Clarity

Cloudy beer should never be bottled. All beer for bottling should be previously fined to prove its clarity. The only permissible clouding is that due to "krausen" wort which is added to the bottle to initiate fermentation for natural conditioning. It is unusual to find a hazy beer that will keep well.

Even yeast primed bottled beer should be visibly clearing within 8 hours after bottling. As gas is given off, it dissolves in the beer, pushing the yeast out of suspension, so that after a day or so, the beer should have reverted back to its original fined clarity. Small quantities of yeast are continually cycled through the beer by thermal currents and also by the action of gas generation to promote adequate conditioning.

Condition

The amount of condition and the fineness of the bead are closely allied to the period of maturation and also how this time was spent. Immature, poorly managed beers give off an initial burst of large, slow moving bubbles that quickly die away, rather like the performance of lemonade. Artificially carbonated beers suffer to some extent with this problem due to the fact that the gas is injected over a short period of time.

Fine beads of gas are the product of condition being gradually dissolved in the beer. To clarify this point, consider that if all the conditioning gas produced by the secondary fermentation could be released into the beer in one burst. The gas, being lighter than the beer, would rush through the liquid and collect over the surface. Very little would be actually dissolved in the beer. On opening the bottle there would be a loud "pop" as the gas excaped from the surface, but the beer would be flat and lifeless since it is devoid of condition. Left unopened and chilled, the gas would gradually dissolve into the beer aided by the circulation of thermal currents. The colder the beer, the more readily the gas will dissolve, but there is a limit with naturally conditioned beer since the yeast will stop working if the temperature falls too low. Ideally the beer is best stored in the coldest temperature that will still permit the yeast to work. For top fermenting yeasts the bottom limit is about 50°F, and about 35°F for the bottom fermenting varieties. By just keeping the yeast just ticking over the amount of gas given off is minimal. Small bubbles rise up through the beer very much slower than larger ones and thus stand a better chance of being retained in solution. Being small they are more widely dispersed which also helps in promoting a fine bead.

The condition released from slow fermenting dextrins in the malt is, by the same reasoning, much better than sucrose for producing fine bead conditioning.

Head formation

The formation of a frothy head on a beer results from the de-pressurising of the carbon dioxide gas in the beer. A "flat" beer cannot produce a head. Pouring or drawing beer from bottles or casks releases the compressed gas to atmospheric pressure. The released gas rises up through the beer in bubbles. Each bubble becomes coated with a skin of low molecular weight degraded protein matter from malt albumin together with dextrins and other gummy substances. At the surface, the bubbles with their filmy coating accumulate to provide the frothy head. Once formed, the head immediately starts to collapse as the suspended beer drains back and the small bubbles combine into larger ones and burst.

Head retention

Head retention is an expression of the time taken for the froth on the surface of the beer to subside. The rate of collapse is largely governed by the constituents and viscosity of the head, the amount of dissolved gas and the bubble size. Head formation is not the same as head retention.

The viscous nature of the dextrins and gums that enclose the gas bubbles, although not actually contributing to the formation of the head, do arrest the collapse of the foam. It must be remembered that most of these products that enhance the head retention properties of beer are *formed by the end of the mashing process* and are thus in the beer at the time of bottling.

Therefore, probably the two most important aspects of brewing technique affecting the amount of these substances that are present in the beer are to ensure that mashing times are not too short, and the pH value of the mash not too high. The use of fresh, high alpha hops is also said to assist foam stability.

A lasting head is often achieved only after a suitable long maturation. The fine gas bead conditioning acquired through the storage of the beer is a major factor in maintaining the

198

frothy head. Closeness of the viscous coating around the small sized bubbles creates a creamy compact head that gives extra mechanical strength and stability to the foam. This characteristic is not attained in an immature beer where the large bubbles readily burst to initiate the destruction of the head.

Commercially, a fine creamy head can be achieved by supplementing the conditioning with another inert gas that is not so soluble in beer as carbon dioxide. The gas is injected and forced into solution. Basically the principle is that the harder the gas is to get in solution, the longer it will take to come out. The slow release of fine gas gives the creamy textured head that will last for hours.

Household detergents and food product greases left in or introduced to the drinking vessel will destroy the head on a beer more quickly than any of the natural processes.

Heading liquids

The formation and retention of the head can sometimes be rather a hit or miss affair. A "headless" beer looks incomplete and unattractive and has consequently led to the widespread use in the commercial field of artificial heading liquids. These aids have the advantage of an assured head that is completely stable and not affected by detergents and fats. Since most home-brewed beer seems to be served from glasses that have not been thoroughly cleansed of these substances, heading liquids can be used with advantage.

Also most home brewers only have a limited storage capacity and thus are not in a position adequately to mature all their beers. In these circumstances I think that the use of heading liquids is perfectly justified and should not be regarded as cheating.

Quick-maturing draught beers should in most cases be treated to a dose of heading liquid to promote a lively head. It would be sacrilege, though, to use these agents in a best bitter drawn from the wood.

More care has got to be exercised when using these liquids in bottled beer. If you use the recommended dose with some of the brands, there is a tendency that you will end up with a batch of fire extinguisher bottles rather than a batch of beer!

199

A third of the recommended dose has proved about right for all beer that is going to be drunk before reaching full maturity.

Storage time

The clarity, condition, and head retention develop to perfection over a period of time. A rough estimation of the time needed to attain this perfection can be made by observing the racking gravity for the secondary fermentation.

For each degree of secondary gravity allow 1 week's maturation. A beer with a starting gravity of 40, for instance, racked off at the quarter gravity stage at a S.G. of 10 for secondary fermentation, will require 10 weeks' maturation. Another racked off at a S.G. of 8 will take 8 weeks' and so on.

Average strength home-brewed beer will keep sound for many months. Usually the flavour of the beer deteriorates and becomes unpalatable before the beer can actually be regarded as being "off". The shelf life is often a reflection of the alcoholic strength and the hop rate. Barley Wines and Strong Ales need 1 to 2 years' maturation before they are ready for drinking. One commercial strong ale is even guaranteed to be at least 25 years old before it reaches the counter.

CHAPTER 28

Rewards

Serving and drinking

SUPPING your home-brewed ale is the reward of this fascinating hobby. Being able to serve a well-made beer to your family and friends brings pride, satisfaction and encouragement for your efforts.

The presentation of the served beer will have a considerable influence on how much it is enjoyed. A good beer can be transformed into a dull, uninteresting, mediocre drink if it is not presented well. A good example of this point is at some outdoor functions when the beer is served in plastic cups.

It is the initial visual impact of the served beer that sets the senses to enticement or rejection. Indeed, there is a lot of truth in the saying that "people drink with their eyes". Even if the beer is found to taste nice, it will not be enjoyed so much if its looks cannot match its flavour.

Beer must look appetising. It should be clear and sparkling, with a good bead and a fine head. Amateur brewers generally do not pay enough attention to serving their wares. In evidence, a pint of beer in a pub usually looks far more inviting than a home-brewed pint. Just for the sake of a little more care and "know how", these common defects and bad practices can easily be overcome.

Drinking vessels

Any container that is watertight and of sensible capacity can be used for serving beer. Glasses, tankards, pewter mugs are the favourites. Under certain circumstances or emergencies, the slippers of fair buxom maidens, or tea cups can be found more appropriate or suitable. I have vague recollections of beer being served at the latter stages of a party from a teapot! My thoughts on how the beer tasted are as hazy as the occasion.

As far as I am concerned, nothing shows off the attributes of a good home-brewed beer than a plain, well polished glass. Again, it is the visual aspect that is most pleasing and comforting in so much that you can see what you are drinking. Served in pewter mugs, or other opaque drinking vessels much of the character of the beer is lost and hidden. Although the beer is usually just as good, its attributes have been unable to visually prime the senses for enticing a thirst.

Glasses must be scrupulously clean. The most displeasing and common fault with serving beer is dirty glasses. When dry a glass can look really clean, but filled, trace deposits can be magnified by the action of the beer.

The inside surface of the glass will hook and retain the rising condition gas. The tiny beads of gas accumulate into large ugly bubbles that stick inside the glass marring and creating a false impression as to the clarity and condition. An accompanying defect from this same source is a rapid destruction of the foam head. IF BUBBLES CLING TO THE SIDE OF THE GLASS, THEN THE GLASS IS DIRTY.

A glass clear of beer stains can still be regarded as dirty. When held up to the light, whitish smears from grease or fingerprints will be seen. All these deposits must be removed by thoroughly washing in a hot detergent solution. Household detergents, however, can have a similar effect to grease in destroying the head of the beer. The use of these liquids is really the lesser of two evils. So long as the glass is thoroughly rinsed to remove all the traces of detergent, the beer will not suffer. I run the glasses under the hot tap, draining and drying 3 times, to ensure that all harmful substances have been removed.

Finally, the glass should be polished with a clean dry cloth especially reserved for this duty. A barman's habit of polishing glasses is a reflection of the importance of clean glasses; and not as many people think, only a job to fill slack periods.

202

Shape of glasses

The shape of the beer glass should be selected to suit the beer. The clarity, condition, bouquet, head retention and temperature must be considered so as to create the right effect and environment for showing the beer to its best advantage.

The degree of carbonation is the major influence on the dimensions of the glass. "Gassy" beers, such as Lagers and Pale Ales need to be chilled to about 45–50°F to accentuate the zest and crispness of the palate and also to retain the natural condition. Tall narrow glasses show off the fine bead conditioning and help to promote a deep foam head. The thick pile of foam affords some protection from the bombarding effect of the gas bubbles which can sometimes disperse the head.

Darker beers are more heavily flavoured and normally lightly carbonated. The flavour is smoother due to less dissolved gas, and the ingredients naturally give a better head retention. Serving temperatures can therefore be slightly warmer than for light beers, but preferably not exceeding 60°F. Glasses can be shallower with a wider mouth, to give ample room for a nice thickness of foam.

Bottled beer

Bottled beer will have a slight yeast deposit thrown by the natural bottle conditioning. To pour a clear beer, this deposit must be left behind in the bottle. The release of gas pressure when the bottle is opened will cause a disturbance that will tend to lift the yeast, creating clouding. Obviously it is very desirable to manage the production of the beer so that there is the minimum of deposited yeast, and that its nature is such that it will tend to adhere to the bottom of the bottle. Good techniques in these matters will allow all but the last $\frac{1}{2}$ in. of beer to be poured clear. The remaining cloudy beer is accepted wastage and must be discarded.

All the clear contents of a bottle must be poured off immediately the bottle is opened. The bottle must be tilted slowly towards the glass without a rocking motion to ensure that the draining takes place with the minimum of yeast disturbance.

Larger bottles, such as quart flagons, can be partially emptied so long as the remainder is left a couple of days for the yeast to settle before it is opened again. A word of warning here, regarding gas pressure: half filled bottles can generate a tremendous pressure of gas. Gas will in preference compress into an "airspace" rather than the beer. The gas will come out of solution when the pressure is released, i.e. when the bottle is opened to atmospheric pressure. In a half filled bottle, there is about 10 times the normal airspace and hence will contain 10 times the usual amount of gas. When the bottle is opened then, this gas is released *immediately* with 10 times the normal force. The ejection can turn the partially loosened stopper into a dangerous projectile: so be careful.

It is a very good habit to wash out the bottle immediately after use to remove all the yeast deposits that could lead to the infection later on, or extra effort in a bottle washing session.

Lively beer

During hot weather, especially with really mature or over primed beer, the beer may expand its wrath in a cascade of foam. The beer is just not manageable under these conditions and it is a fair bet that if one bottle displays this characteristic, then the whole batch will be similarly affected. The treatment is dependent on the stopper. If a screw stopper is used on the bottle, then all that is needed is to quickly twist the closure to break the seal, vent the airspace pressure and twist close again before fobbing can commence. Implement this treatment for all the bottles and repeat over a day or so until the pressure is normal. No beer should be wasted by this procedure.

Plastic reseals and crown caps are a little more difficult. It is not a practical proposition to try the vent/reseal technique with these closures. Chilling the beer first might work with the plastic reseals, though, but I doubt if your skill as a "Beer Remueur" could match those of your wine counterpart in the champagne cellars.

The best idea is to pour all the bottles into a pressure barrel and fit the injector unit with its integral safety valve. The beer can then be left for a few days and used as draught or primed again and rebottled.

Draught beer

The temperature of serving draught can be about 5°
higher than for the same type of bottled beer. Always give
a full measure of draught beer, and not limit the quantity
to the amount that will fill the glass without the foam fobbing
over. The glass must always be filled with beer to within
$\frac{1}{2}$–$\frac{3}{4}$ in. of the rim to give the right texture of head. Ideally,
the glass should be filled with the tap outlet below the surface
of the beer and the level raised to overflow the fluffy foam to
just leave a creamy head topping the beer.

Eurokeg and Sparklet systems with their constant low
pressure ejections are superb in giving the beer the fine creamy
nead that is associated with the best commercial beers.

Problems

"Some . . . troubles are bound to be experienced"

THE brewing of beer is a very simple process, but for all its ease, some failures and troubles are bound to be experienced. Nearly always, the reasons for these upsets can be identified and remedial action taken. The farther through the brewing process these faults occur, the more serious the defects tend to become, and the less chance there is of correcting them.

Experience is gained through mistakes, and I feel that a measure of failure is worthwhile in the long run in establishing priorities rather than learning all the techniques from the book.

I have tried in these previous chapters to highlight all the pitfalls and sources of trouble. Below is a summary of the most likely sources of problems, discussed in the order in which they are often encountered.

Yeast starters

Always plan the preparation of the yeast starter some time ahead of the main brew. Judgement is best made on the cultivation period based on previous experience, so that when the main brew is ready, the yeast is ripe for pitching. There should always be vigorous activity in the starter before an attempt is made to start the main brew. If not, delay the brewing session until the starter is ready. Never be impatient over this matter. A cooled wort left dormant just cannot be adequately protected, even by an airtight cover. Adding another yeast to a slow starter may cause incompatibility that can result in poor fermentation, flavour, and clarity.

Mashing

Mashing is one of the stages in brewing that affords very little latitude for carelessness and inattention. The first few minutes of mashing are extremely critical regarding the temperature of the goods.

The temperature of the mixing water, known as the strike heat, is high enough in itself to destroy the malt enzymes. Preventing the destruction of enzymes is secured by efficiently and quickly mixing the water with the cool grains to bring the temperature down to around 150°F. Stabilisation of the heat can only be achieved after a couple of minutes of continual stirring.

The stiff mixture will quite often give an erroneous reading. A range between 140 and 160°F. can be recorded in various positions and depths in the mash. There is a natural urgency at this stage to make adjustments on the assumption that the heat has stabilised.

It can be very difficult to reverse a hasty decision made on temperature adjustment. The whole success of the subsequent processes hinges on these few moments, so make absolutely certain that the mash requires adjusting before adding any extra water.

Low extracts

A sample of the wort collected after sparging must always be tested to determine the extract from the mashed grain. Using the Degrees of Extract system (chapter 19), determine the efficiency of mashing. All the recipes in this book have been designed assuming maximum extract from the malt (i.e. 30 degrees for each pound of mashed grain). If for instance only an 80 per cent extraction was achieved from a mash (80% × 30 = 24 degrees per lb.) then the weight of hops, sugar and the length of beer must also be reduced by 80 per cent. In this case to maintain the balance of ingredients, only 4 gallons of beer would be made from a 5 gallon recipe. NEVER RESTORE THE FERMENTABLE EXTRACT WITH SUGAR TO COMPENSATE FOR A LOW MASHED EXTRACT.

From my experience, 9 out of 10 cases of low extracts are due to inefficient or insufficient sparging of the mashed grain. If sparging has been implemented correctly, and Starch End Point passed, then probably a sample of poor quality malt has found its way into your brewing store.

Sparging

The major problem that occurs with sparging is the set mash. Malt crushed too fine is usually the cause of this condition which allows the malt flour to form a paste at the bottom of the mash tun and block the flow of sweet wort. Sparging too fast can also cause this condition. The solution

208

to the problem is to close the tap and stir the mash for about a minute. After another few minutes rest, sparging can usually be successfully restarted.

Boiling

The equipment in hand can cause restrictions. Ideally, all the wort must be boiled with the hops and sugar. These requirements can pose problems when, for instance, you wish to brew a 5 gallon batch with only a 2 or 3 gallon boiler. The procedure is simple. Just boil the first fraction of sparged wort with the hops. Most of the gravity will be extracted in the first gallon or two, so nearly all the benefits of boiling can still be achieved.

The remaining worts can be collected and boiled separately with the sugar. Ten minutes of boiling will usually break the small amount of remaining protein matter out of suspension. This second wort can then be added to the dustbin together with the first.

Fermentation

Luckily, most of us do not possess a microscope. If we did, we would probably never be satisfied with our yeast nor the fermentation! The list of ills that can befall the poor yeast are innumerable. On the finer points "Ignorance is bliss", and visual checks are sufficient to give a guide to the performance and efficiency of the yeast.

Fermentation should be conducted at a steady pace, not too slow nor too fast. The major influence on this factor is the temperature which should be kept between 55 and 65°F. Provided a yeast crop is covering the surface of the brew, then fermentation is best conducted at the lower temperature. Poor yeasts will often attenuate the beer at the same rate as a good one. Some inferior yeasts do not have the ability to create the protective pancake type head, and instead just produce large, oily bubbles. A lack of nutrients, especially with low gravity, low malt content beers, can also produce this effect.

Fast "racing" fermentations are also best avoided. Acceleration of the fermentation due to higher temperatures can increase the risk of infection. All beer worts contain harmful bacteria that are normally kept dormant by the low fermentation temperatures, until they are killed by the alcohol produced by the yeast. Temperatures above 77°F can activate these spoilage organisms that can ruin the beer before and *after* the yeast has taken a hold.

Lack of attenuation resulting in the primary fermentation abating at specific gravities above the quarter stage is probably due to a bad maltose/dextrin ratio stemming from an excess amount of dextrins, caused by too high a mash temperature or too short a mashing period.

Low secondary specific gravities are conversely due to low mash temperatures or prolonged mash times that favour the production of maltose. Incorrect pH values of the mash will also alter these gravity readings.

The finished beer

Millions of pounds are spent every year by the professional brewers in their research into the defects that can occur in the finished beer. The research is leading to a far better understanding of the processes of brewing and their findings gradually percolate down to our amateur circles. We do not have their equipment nor facilities for accurate diagnosis of beer disorders and hence our judgement must be made using our basic human senses and practical experience. We can only apply these skills to recognising the basic diseases, since we really cannot expect to identify, let alone diagnose the more obscure brewery infections. For this reasoning, discussion on this topic must obviously be limited.

"Flat" beer

A "flat" beer results from the absence of conditioning gas that leaves the beer "still" and devoid of "fizz". A lack of conditioning gas may result from having insufficient dextrinous or priming sugar in the beer. Immature beers will lack condition and using a weak yeast or storing the bottles at too low a temperature are also contributing factors for this condition. Sometimes the gas is produced but escapes. The loss of conditioning gas can be avoided by using new plastic reseals for each bottling session and also ensuring that the rubber washers on the screw stoppers are in good order. Perished and old washers must be replaced.

210

No head

Quite often a lack of head retention is due to insufficient conditioning gas. A flat beer cannot promote nor retain a good foam. Grease and detergents are the worst enemies of head retention. These substances must be avoided where possible in *all* equipment and utensils; and not just the drinking vessels. High gravity beers tend to have a better head retention than the weaker types because of the higher malt and hop contents.

HAZES

Yeast haze

So long as there is fermentable sugar in the beer, active brewery yeasts will remain in suspension. Far more yeast will remain in suspension than is actually needed to complete the fermentation; this is why it is recommended practice to fine and Krausen the beer to reduce the amount of conditioning yeast to a minimum. Clear beer is easy to achieve with brewery yeast, but if turbidity is experienced then wild yeasts may have found their way into your brew. One strain of yeast, Sacch. Diastaticus can ferment the dextrins far more readily than the normal S. cerevisiae types and consequently can cause problems, especially with bottled beers.

Starch haze

Starch hazes can be avoided so long as mashing is prolonged passed the Starch End Point as determined by the iodine test. If there is still discolouration of the iodine after 1½ hours' mashing, more diastase must be added to the mashtun by stirring in a cupful of diastatic malt extract syrup. Check first that the temperature and pH of the mash is sympathetic to starch conversion processes before adding the syrup.

Protein haze

The problems of hazes caused by nitrogenous matter are very complex. Creating the best environment for preventing hazes from one group of substances can often increase the haze risk from others. Seemingly, it is difficult

211

to strike a complete satisfactory balance. The common causes of protein haze are inadequate degradation of these nitrogenous substances during mashing and insufficient boiling of the wort. Practically we can do very little about a protein haze in the *finished* beer (except drink it from an opaque beer mug!). If you are lucky, the haze will sometimes precipitate out of the beer during storage. On the other hand, a clear beer kept under the same storage conditions can throw a haze—you just cannot win! The frequency of this happening is quite small if sound brewing techniques are used with well-balanced recipes.

Chill haze

Chill hazes, as their name implies, are experienced in beers that are cooled before serving. Lagers kept in the refrigerator are very prone to this trouble. The reaction is reverisible and the haze will disappear as the beer warms up again. Globulin and tannin based substances are usually the culprits in this clouding, which is best avoided by adopting the methods recommended for protein hazes.

Disease

Beer is a low-acid, low-alcohol drink produced from sugary malt solutions and thus provides a fertile source for the incubation of spoilage organisms.

The acetic acid and the lactic acid bacteria are the most common sources of brewery infections and they, as their names imply, also increase the acidity of the beer. "Vinegar Bug" as the acetic acid bacteria is commonly called by homebrewers, can only flourish in the presence of air. Before and after the fermentation ceases are the danger times. Using pure yeast, pitching working starters and taking care to exclude air during racking can minimise the problem. A distinctive smell of vinegar and taste of the same, if you wish to risk it, are the obvious symptoms of an attack from this bacteria.

Certain wild yeast also flourish in the presence of air to form a powdery deposit on the surface of the brew. Left unchecked the mould forms a whitish, crinkled crust covering the surface of the beer.

212

There are two types of lactic acid bacteria which may be recognised in our beers. The first is the rod type which will cause the beer to display a silky sheen when swirled in the bottle and will pour like thin engine oil. Ropiness, the second consideration, is caused by another bacteria which is classed with the former since its infecting action also produces lactic acid.

This bacteria will result in the beer having a thick, viscous constituency, that does indeed look like rope or thick cord when it is poured from the bottle. In bad cases it has been reported that the beer will set into a thick gel inside the bottle.

Infected beer must always be discarded and the containers and utensils that have been in contact with it must be thoroughly sterilised with the "bleach" treatment to minimise the risk of a repeated performance in subsequent brews.

CHAPTER 30

Pale ales

PALE ALE represents the very best in English beer. It is a high-gravity, light-coloured beer, generously hopped, with a dry crisp taste that complements the heavy carbonation. No other type of beer reflects so well the quality of the ingredients. The finest quality hops, with a good rub and aroma, and the best of the well-modified English malts are reserved for these special ales.

The proportion of adjuncts should also be kept to a minimum, and only be sufficient to balance the malt nitrogen so as not to distract from the "maltiness" of the brew. Large amounts of sugar must also be discouraged for the same reasons.

A long maturation in the bottle is necessary to bring the beer to its best. Mashing temperatures are slightly higher than usual in order to produce a dextrinous wort capable of issuing secondary conditioning gas in the bottle over a long storage period.

PREMIUM PALE ALE

Ingredients for 5 gallons at a S.G. of 48

  7 lb. Crushed pale malt
  5 oz. Flaked rice
  1 oz. Cracked crystal malt
  1 lb. Demerara sugar
  2 oz. Goldings hops
  ½ oz. Progress hops
  Top fermenting beer yeast.

Production information

Follow the basic method as given in chapter 3.

Mashing water	Permanently hard with the minimum of carbonates
Mash pH	5·0–5·3, adjust with Gypsum
Water temperatures	Mix at 168–170°F to give an initial heat of 150–152°F.
Mashing time	3 hours or overnight
Sparged wort	Collect 6 gallons and check that the S.G. is 36
Maximum possible extract	220 degrees
Hops	Select to 13 A.A.U.'s
Boiling	Add Irish Moss for last ½ hour of 1½–2 hour boil
Final collected quantity	5¼ gallons at S.G. of 48
Racking gravity	S.G. of 11–12.

"RED PENNANT" PALE ALE

Ingredients for 4 gallons at a S.G. of 44

> 5 lb. Crushed pale malt
> 5 oz. Flaked barley
> 2 oz. Crushed wheat malt
> 3 oz. East Kent Goldings hops
> 1 lb. Demerara sugar
> Top fermenting beer yeast.

Production information

Follow the basic method.

Water and treatment	As per Premium P.A. recipe
Mashing time	3 hours or overnight
Sparged wort	Collect 4½ gallons at S.G. 35
Maximium possible extract	160 degrees
Hops	Select to 15 A.A.U.'s
Boiling	Add Irish Moss for last ½ hour of 1½–2 hour boil
Final collected quantity	4¼ gallons at S.G. 44
Racking gravity	S.G. of 10–11.

"CRESTA" PALE ALE

Ingredients for 4½ gallons at a S.G. of 49

7 lb. Crushed pale malt
¾ lb. Demerara sugar
2 oz. Hallertau hops
1¼ oz. Goldings hops *or* ¾ oz. OT 48 hops
Top fermenting beer yeast.

Production information—Follow the basic method.

Water and treatment	As per the Premium P.A. recipe
Mashing time	3 hours or overnight
Sparged wort	Collect 5¼ gallons at S.G. 40
Maximum possible extract	210 degrees
Hops	Select to 18 A.A.U.'s
Boiling	Add Irish Moss to last ½ hour of 1½–2 hour boil
Final collected quantity	4¾ gallons at S.G. 49
Racking gravity	S.G. of 11–12.

"SIXES AND SEVENS"

Ingredients for 4 gallons at a S.G. of 55

6 lb. Crushed pale malt
6 oz. Brewing flour
7 oz. Soft brown sugar
7 oz. White sugar
3 oz. Goldings or W.G.V. hops.
½ oz. W.G.V. or OT 48 hops
Top fermenting beer yeast.

Production information—Follow the basic method

Water and treatment	As per Premium P.A. recipe
Mashing time	3 hours or overnight
Sparged wort	Collect 4½ gallons at S.G. 42
Maximum possible extract	190 degrees
Hops	Select to 19 A.A.U.'s
Boiling	Add Irish Moss for the last ½ hour of 1½–2 hour boil
Final collected quantity	4 gallons at S.G. of 55
Racking gravity	S.G. of 14–15.

CHAPTER 31

Light ales

LIGHT ALES are clean refreshing beers and ideal thirst quenchers. In many ways they are similar to a light gravity Pale Ale. The hop rate is obviously lower than for Pale Ales, but it is nevertheless commensurate with the malt content. Light flavour and heavy carbonation again bring out best in good quality hops. Flaked adjuncts can be used with advantage in these ales, so long as the yeast nutrient properties of the wort are not diluted too much. Maturation time should be fairly short which favours the use of household sugars in the formulation. Too much sugar though, will produce a beer that is thin and lacking in body.

Mashing temperatures of 150°F, yield a satisfactory ratio of malt sugars. The inclusion of Irish Moss to give a better "break" condition is not so necessary as with Pale Ales on account that the malt and protein content is much lower.

FIRST LIGHT

Ingredients for 5 gallons at a S.G. of 35

4 lb. Crushed pale malt
1½ lb. White sugar
2 oz. Goldings hops
½ oz. OT 48 or Progress hops
Top fermenting beer yeast.

217

Production information

Follow the basic method given in chapter 3.

Water	Medium to hard water containing a minimum amount of carbonates.
Mash pH	5·0–5·2, adjust with Gypsum and Epsom salts.
Water temperatures	Mix at 168–170°F. to give an initial heat of 150°F
Mashing time	2–3 hours or overnight
Sparged wort	Collect 5 gallons at S.G. 24
Maximum possible extract	120 degrees
Hops	Select to 12 A.A.U.'s
Boiling	Boil 1½–2 hours. Add Irish Moss for short boiling times.
Final collected quantity	Top up to 5 gallon at S.G. of 35
Racking gravity	S.G. of 6–7.

"STARBRIGHT" LIGHT ALE

Ingredients for 5 gallons at S.G. of 39

> 5 lb. Crushed pale malt
> 12 oz. Flaked rice
> 1 lb. Soft brown sugar
> 1½ oz. Hallertau hops
> ½ oz. Goldings hops
> Top fermenting beer yeast.

Production information

Method as for First Light recipe except:

Sparged wort	Collect 5½ gallons at S.G. 31
Maximum possible extract	170 degrees
Hops	Select to 13 A.A.U.'s
Final collected quantity	5¼ gallons at S.G. of 39
Racking gravity	S.G. of 7–8.

"CHALLENGER" LIGHT ALE

Ingredients for 5 gallons at a S.G. of 39

5 lb. Crushed pale malt
8 oz. Brewing flour
3 oz. Flaked rice
1 lb. Demerara sugar
3 oz. Goldings hops
Top fermenting beer yeast.

Production information

Method as for First light recipe except:

Sparged wort	Collect 5½ gallons at S.G. 31
Maximum possible extract	170 degrees
Hops	Select to 15 A.A.U.'s
Final collected quantity	5¼ gallons at S.G. of 39
Racking gravity	S.G. of 8–9.

"44" LIGHT

Ingredients for 4 gallons at a S.G. of 35

4 lb. Crushed pale malt
4 oz. Flaked barley
4 oz. Flaked maize
4 oz. Demerara sugar
4 oz. White sugar
1½ oz. Goldings hops
½ oz. Progress hops
Top fermenting beer yeast.

Production information

Method as per First light recipe except:

Sparged wort	Collect 4¾ gallons at S.G. 28
Maximum possible extract	135 degrees
Hops	Select to 11 A.A.U.'s
Final collected quantity	4¼ gallons at S.G. of 35
Racking gravity	S.G. of 6–7.

CHAPTER 32

Bitters

BITTER is the favourite beer in our fair land. It is as English as "fish and chips", and can be regarded as the "beer ordinaire" of the drinking man. Bitter performs so much better on draught than in the bottle. The formulation is very much like that of Pale Ale, and indeed, some commercial breweries take the worts from the same mash-tun and just use more hops with the Pale Ale beers.

The notable difference in the finished beers is the final gravity. Bitters are usually far sweeter, presenting a smoother bodied, fuller flavoured beer. Specialised brewing sugars are extremely useful for bitter production, since they can be manufactured to leave any desired percentage of unfermentables in the beer. As yet, these commercial sugars are taking a long time to percolate down to our end of the trade. Dark household sugars, such as Demerara and Barbados, are the home brewer's compromise, even although these only impart residual flavour and very little unfermentables.

Mashing at higher temperatures than normal can produce the requisite degree of sweetness for draught bitter. The colour of the beer should shade between a light and dark golden. I am rather bemused that the commercial bitters have been progressively darkened over the last decade as the original gravities have fallen. Seemingly, darkening the beer gives the illusion of strength. After all, caramel is cheaper than alcohol!

"BREWER'S REWARD"

A high class, strong bitter, typical of the excellent ales of long ago, designed as a draught beer for use in pressure barrels or from the "wood".

Ingredients for 5½ gallons at S.G. of 45

7 lb. Crushed pale malt
8 oz. Cracked crystal malt
5 oz. Cracked wheat malt
12 oz. Demerara sugar
3 oz. Goldings hops
1 oz. Bramling Cross *or* Progress hops
Top fermenting beer yeast.

Production information

Follow the basic method given in chapter 3.

Water	Moderately hard with not too high a proportion of carbonates
Mash pH	5·0–5·2 adjust with Gypsum and Potassium chloride
Water temperatures	Mix at 168–170°F to give an initial heat of 150–152°F.
Mashing time	3 hours or overnight
Sparged wort	Collect 6½ gallons at S.G. 36
Maximum possible extract	234 degrees
Hops	Select to 22 A.A.U.'s
Boiling	1½–2 hours. Add Irish Moss for last half hour.
Final quantity	5¾ gallons at a S.G. of 45
Racking graity	S.G. of 11–12.

CRYSTAL BITTER

An easy made bitter with a beautiful golden colour. This recipe is my stock "drinking" bitter, and it has a good flavour expecially when enhanced with a few Bullion hops.

Just using a small handful (say a dozen cones), of these hops gives the beer a distinct, yet pleasant bite.

Ingredients for 5 gallons at a S.G. of 42

6 lb. Crushed pale malt
½ lb. Cracked crystal malt
1 lb. Demerara sugar
2 oz. Goldings hops
1 oz. Fuggles plus Bullion hops
Top fermenting beer yeast.

Production information

Method as per Brewer's Reward recipe except:

Sparged wort	Collect 6 gallons at S.G. 32
Maximum possible extract	190 degrees
Hops	Select to 17 A.A.U.'s
Final collected quantity	5¼ gallons at a S.G. of 42
Racking gravity	S.G. of 9–10.

BLACK KNIGHT BITTER

Another tasty beer to brew is my Black Knight bitter, in which a small quantity of black malt is used. It is drier than usual for the type and quite crisp. The dark amber colour contrasts well with the white creamy head.

Ingredients for 5 gallons at a S.G. of 48

6 lb. Crushed pale malt
¾ lb. Cracked crystal malt
1 oz. Cracked black malt
1½ lb. White sugar
2½ oz. Goldings hops
½ oz. British Columbian seedless Goldings hops
½ oz. Fuggles hops
Top fermenting beer yeast.

Production information

Method as per Brewer's Reward recipe except:

Sparged wort	Collect 6 gallons at S.G. 33
Maximum possible extract	195 degrees
Hops	Select to 20 A.A.U.'s
Final collected quantity	5¼ gallons at a S.G. of 48
Racking gravity	S.G. of 9–10.

"BODY" BITTER

Ingredients for 5 gallons at a S.G. of 50

    7 lb. Crushed pale malt
    4 oz. Flaked maize
    4 oz. Cracked crystal malt
    4 oz. Torrefied barley
    1 lb. Glucose chips
    2 oz. Goldings hops
    1 oz. Hallertau hops
    Top fermenting beer yeast.

Production information

Method as per Brewer's Reward recipe except:

Sparged wort	Collect 6 gallons at S.G. 38
Maximum possible extract	230 degrees
Hops	Select to 18 A.A.U.'s
Final collected quantity	5¼ gallons at a S.G. of 50.

"LIGHT BITTER"

Ingredients for 5 gallons at a S.G. of 37

    5 lb. Crushed pale malt
    6 oz. Flaked rice
    1 Dessertspoonful of Gravy Browning
    1 lb. White sugar
    2½ oz. Goldings hops
    ½ oz. Progress hops.
    Top fermenting beer yeast.

Production information

Method as per Brewer's Reward recipe except:

Sparged wort	Collect 5½ gallons at S.G. 29
Maximum possible extract	160 degrees
Hops	Select to 16 A.A.U.'s
Final collected quantity	5¼ gallons at a S.G. of 37
Racking gravity	S.G. of 7–8.

CHAPTER 33

Lagers

LAGER is rapidly becoming one of the most popular drinks in the country. The rise in favour from almost total obscurity a decade ago, must admittedly be due to the power of mass advertising, and also to the deterioration of our English ales. But on a hot summer's day, nothing can match the thirst-quenching properties of a cool, draught lager.

Lager is known to most people as a very pale coloured beer, that is heavily carbonated and served chilled to accentuate its clean refreshing flavour. Only this type has been promoted in this country with any real success. Lagers, though, are a whole family of beers ranging from the light delicate Pilsen beers, to the dark, aromatic Munich types, and thus they can only really be categorised by the common brewing system used in their production.

Nearly all the ingredients and processes used in the brewing of lager show some marked difference to their counterparts in the production of our English top fermenting ales.

It is the ingredients of beer, mainly the barley malt, that initially decides whether the brewing process will follow an English infusion mash or a continental decoction mash system. Continental malts are mainly derived from six rowed barleys, which on balance, are regarded as being inferior to the English two rowed barley. The decoction system is designed to extract every ounce of goodness from these poorer malts.

I always refer to lager malt as being "underdone" both in the germination and the drying processes of malting. The undermodified state ensured that the germinating seed of barley does not grow to infringe the region that would bring about a loss of extract. The important side effect of this policy is that the stunted growth of the embryo plant results in a surplus of unwanted nitrogen based plant food in the grain kernel. Certain constituent parts of these nutrient products, collectively termed the nitrogen content, will cause irreversible hazes if passed through to the finished beer.

It is this characteristic that demands that lager malt must be mashed by a decoction system. The first part of a decoction mash is solely devoted to changing the excess nitrogen into a form that can be removed in the subsequent stages in the brewing chain.

Returning to the malting, the temperature of the drying air is kept as low as possible to prevent roasting of the malt husk. Low colouring of the husks is essential for preserving the pale colour of the beer.

Another factor of this low heat treatment is that the destruction of useful enzymes, such as diastase, is minimised. High nitrogen, high Linter malt is ideal for employing with large proportions of unmalted adjuncts. American beers, especially, make full use of this economic characteristic, and employ large quantities of flakes.

Water for Lager

The water for making beer has always got to be matched to the malt grist to effect the best reactions during mashing. The main considerations of water treatment for Lager production are the preservation of the delicate flavour and colour of the beer. Salts that contribute to temporary hardness are definitely not wanted, and must be avoided at all costs. Calcium carbonate, in particular, gives a reddish hue to the beer. Carbonates also impart a harshness that can ruin the delicacy of the continental hops. Soft water then, complements lager malt, and the low salt content balances the natural high acidity of these malts. Lager can quite easily be made from ordinary English pale malt so long as the pH of the mash is adjusted with Gypsum. Lager is therefore peculiar in so much that it can be brewed from soft or permanently hard water, depending on the type of malt used in the grist.

Lager Yeast

Brewery yeasts can be divided into four classes depending on their fermentation characteristics. Class 1 are bottom fermenters, and Class 1 are top fermenters, with Classes 2 and 3 biasing towards their associated extremes. Lager yeasts are the Class 4 type and are also a pure strain. A pure strain of yeast that works from the bottom is the perfect combination for our naturally conditioned beer.

Although lager yeast finally sinks to the bottom of the fermentation vessel, it will still throw a yeast crop on the surface of the brew for the first few days. It is not such a spectacular performance as is witnessed with a top fermenter. A rocky head of yeast is sometimes experienced, but it usually gives way to a light fluffy head, somewhat reminiscent of the frothy head that tops a freshly poured lager.

Closed fermentation

The lack of surface activity is rather aggravated by the lower temperatures used for lager fermentations. Rarely is the thickness of the primary yeast crop more than one inch. There is also a tendency for the yeast to migrate towards the centre of the surface, leaving the outer edge exposed. Fermenting beer left exposed to the air invites infection, and hence lager fermentations are best conducted in a closed container.

Plastic dustbins with tight fitting lids, or 5 gallon "Ex Wine" polythene cubes are ideal for home-brewed lager. In a true closed container, the surface of the brew is inaccessible and the course of fermentation must progress without any direct interference.

By excluding air, and using low hop rates, the yeast crop is clean and does not require much, if any, skimming. Low temperature fermentation assists this matter by limiting the production of excess yeast.

It is usually quite acceptable to allow the yeast crop, if clean, to drop through the beer after primary fermentation without fear of imparting off flavours.

Low temperature fermentation

To accentuate the delicate flavour and to give a briskness on the palate, lager is highly carbonated. Traditionally, lager

226

is highly saturated with carbon dioxide gas; a secondary effect of the lager yeasts ability to carry on working at low temperatures.

The carbon dioxide gas readily dissolves in the beer, the lower the temperature, the more of the gas can be dissolved.

It is the practice on the Continent to create conditions that are most favourable for the beer to absorb the maximum amount of gas. The temperature of the beer is lowered by refrigeration so that the yeast is only just working. Many lager yeasts are fermented as low as 4°C to prolong the fermentation.

Long storage periods at low temperatures are the only way to produce a traditional naturally conditioned lager beer. In fact, the word "lager" is derived from the German verb "to store".

Obviously, cold fermentations can create problems for the amateur brewer. Trying to persuade your spouse that a 5 gallon barrel of German Lager should have pride of place in the food compartment of your refrigerator for a few months takes some doing!

A reasonably good imitation can be brewed by conducting the fermentation in a garage or outhouse during the winter months.

From my experience, these long tedious continental practices are best forsaken in favour of a limited decoction system, or by simply using pale malt with the infusion mash. Careful attention to the water treatment aspect will usually ensure that the delicacy of flavour and colour are maintained.

Hops for Lager

Only seedless hops are suitable for lager production. The best flavoured varieties, the Saaz and Hallertau, are becoming more plentiful on the home brewing markets, but they are rather more expensive than the English hops. Hopping rates are much lower, which partially offsets the extra cost.

S.L. LAGER
METHOD
Recipe for 5 gallons at a S.G. of 35

5 lb. Lager Malt	1 lb. White sugar
2½ oz. Hallertau hops	Lager yeast.

Boil about 5½ gallons of water for a ¼ hour and then switch off the boiler. Whilst the water is cooling, crush the grain and prepare mash-tun for mashing.

Mashing

When the temperature of the water in the boiler falls to 140°F, open the tap of the boiler and allow the water to fall into the mash-tun. Mix in the crushed grain and stir thoroughly. The ideal consistency is achieved by mixing the 5 lb. of malt with 10 pints of the water, with the net result that the mix should settle out at a temperature of about 125°F. Five degrees either way from this figure does not matter too much. Replace the airtight lid on the mash-tun.

Let the mash stand for ½ hour for the protein digestion to take place. After this initial low temperature mash, move the mash tun and position it on a worktop or safe shelf. Lift off the lid and open the tap of the mash-tun and let the cloudy wort drain into a large saucepan. It should be possible to collect 5 pints of wort by natural drainage from the grains.

Heat up the cloudy wort in the saucepan as quickly as possible to just under boiling point and then return it to the mash-tun, stirring it into the grains as quickly and as thoroughly as possible. The temperature of the "goods" should now have been raised to the saccharification temperature of 150°F. Check the temperature of the mix with a thermometer and adjust if and as necessary with small additions of hot or cold water to bring it to within the range 148–152°F.

Replace the lid on the mash-tun and leave i. for a couple of hours.

After about 1 hour's mashing confirm that saccharification has taken place by testing a sample of the grains with iodine. No bluish-black discolouration should be seen when a few drops of iodine are added to a spoonful of the goods taken from the mash-tun.

After mashing, raise the boiler water temperature to 170°F and transfer all the water above the tap level to a 5 gallon polythene cube for sparging. The last few pints of water left in the boiler contain the precipitated chalk hardness which should be discarded before the boiler is used again for boiling the wort.

Sparge the grain and boil the wort with the sugar and the hops for an hour. Strain the hot wort through the filter bed of hops into a dustbin and finally sparge the hops with 1 kettleful of boiling water to release the remaining extract.

When the wort has cooled to 60°F pitch a working Lager yeast and replace the lid on the dustbin. Ferment in a cool place for a few days until the fluffy yeast head sinks from the surface of the brew. The yeast will now be working mainly from the bottom and should be racked into a closed container and left under an airlock for a week or two to fall bright.

This Lager has been specifically designed to work right out and thus all the conditioning must be derived from white sugar primings. Long maturation for conditioning is consequently not necessary. Ideally, from bottling to drinking, the temperature of the beer should be maintained between 40 and 59°F. Technically, the temperature is governed by the lowest temperature that the yeast you are using will just still work. Kept within this range the beer can take up to three quarters of a level teaspoonful of priming sugar per pint.

Bottled Lager must be chilled before drinking.

"CERVEZA" LAGER

Ingredients for 4 gallons at a S.G. of 45

    5 lb. Crushed lager malt
    1 lb. Flaked maize
    2 oz. Mixed seedless hops
    Lager beer yeast.

Method

Follow the method for "S.L." Lager.

LINESTEIN LAGER

Ingredients for 4 gallons at a S.G. of 45

    6 lb. Crushed lager malt
    2½ oz. Saaz hops
    Lager beer yeast.

Method

Follow the method for "S.L." Lager.

Pale malt

Pale malt may be substituted for lager malt in the above recipes but the pH of the mash will need adjusting with Gypsum to around 5·2. The decoction protein rest is still advisable to prevent a chill haze in the beer when it is cooled prior to drinking.

CHAPTER 34

Mild ales

MILD ALE is one of the most popular beers brewed by the commercial brewers, but is rarely made by the amateur. Up until the late "50's", it accounted for almost half of the beer drunk in this country, but has since declined in popularity in favour of the mass advertised keg bitters. Mild does not perform well as a keg beer, nor does it suit modern cellar practice, and hence it tends to be shunned by the commercial trade. If we do not start brewing our own, I am sure that within a few years it will just be another tradition lost in the march of rationalisation.

Mild Ale is renown for its luscious sweet flavour and thirst quenching properties. The other distinctive characteristic of it is that it is very low in alcoholic strength, and is usually the weakest beer turned out by the breweries.

Mind you, I am not advocating brewing beer as weak as some commercial varieties where the flavour of the mineral salts is more pronounced than that of the malt and hops.

A starting gravity between 38 and 40 degrees would seem about right for a home-brewed Mild Ale. For this fairly low gravity, at least three-quarters of the fermentable extract must be derived from Pale Malt to ensure adequate nutrients for the yeast. A special mild ale malt is available although I have not come across any stocked locally. Obviously it is better to use a malt that has been manufactured to suit this particular type of beer, but I doubt if we would really notice

231

the difference in the finished beer. Mild Ale Malt, which tends to give a fuller flavoured beer, is kilned at a higher temperature and results in a darker coloured malt with a restricted diastatic activity.

The practical implications of using this malt are that it must be mashed at a few degrees lower than normal (i.e. 145–148°F) to coax the best saccharification performance from the diastase enzymes. The darker malt will also partially offset the need for additional colouring matter.

The higher kilning temperature usually results in a slightly lower extract from mashing than can be attained with using Pale Malt. Both types, however, should yield 28–30 degree extracts in the mash-tun. This means that each pound of malt will provide about 30 degrees of specific gravity for each gallon of beer, which for Mild Ale satisfies the required three-quarters of the fermentable extract. The remaining 10 degrees can be extracted from malt adjuncts.

The selection of these malt adjuncts to make up the fermentable sugars is very important. Mild Ale is traditionally a quick maturing beer that is ready for supping only a few days after casking. Being a dark colour obviously also helps in covering up any deficiences in clarity that could arise from such a short casking time.

The maturation time of beer can be shortened by using a fairly high proportion of sugar or another low nitrogen content adjunct in the formulation. A first class Mild Ale can be brewed by just using Pale Malt and sugar alone, but modern palates seem to prefer the use of more grain adjuncts to provide the extra body to balance the low gravity of the beer.

AMAZING MILD ALE

Ingredients for 5 gallons at a S.G. of 35

5 lb. Crushed pale malt
1 lb. Demerara sugar
5 oz. Cracked crystal malt
5 oz. Cracked roast barley
2 oz. Fuggles hops
Top fermenting beer yeast.

Production information

Follow the basic method given in chapter 3.

Water	Soft, with chlorides and Gypsum
Mash pH	5·0–5·2 Adjust with Potassium Chloride or Gypsum
Water temperatures	Mix at 168–170°F to give an initial heat of 150°F
Mashing Time	3 hours or overnight
Sparged wort	Collect 5¾ gallons at S.G. of 27
Maximum possible extract	155 degrees
Hops	Select to 10 A.A.U.'s
Boiling	Boil 1½–2 hours
Final collected quantity	5¼ gallons at a S.G. of 35
Racking gravity	S.G. of 7–8.

MIDLANDS MILD ALE

Ingredients for 5 gallons at a S.G. of 35

5 lb. Crushed pale malt
5 oz. Cracked black malt
5 oz. Cracked roast barley
2 oz. Cracked torrefied barley
1 lb. Dark sugar
2 oz. Fuggles or Northern Brewer hops
Top fermenting beer yeast.

Production information

Method as per Amazing Mild Ale recipe.

CHAPTER 35

Brown ales and sweet stouts

BROWN ALES and sweet stouts are best dealt with together. Both are sweet, dark, heavy bodied bottled beers, and which are never served on draught. The predominant feature of these beers is their strong, luscious flavour derived from the use of roasted grains and sugar caramels. Hops are used merely to support the sweetness of the malt and sugars, and not as a salient flavour as in the case of some lighter beers. Sweetness cannot tolerate too much gas in the beer. Browns, being lighter bodied and drier than stouts, can withstand slightly more carbonation.

The basic brewing method should be followed for making these beers. Additional treatment though, is necessary for the inclusion of the non-fermentable sugars, such as lactose, Sweetex liquid, and caramel colouring agents.

Lactose must be made up into a solution before it is added to the wort for boiling in the copper. When sparging the wort after mashing, draw off a couple of pints for dissolving the lactose: this obviates the need to use additional water that would dilute the brew. Making the sugar up into a solution prevents it being burnt on the bottom of the boiler when it is added to the wort.

The final colour of the beer is also best adjusted during the boiling stage. Remember; the beer can always be darkened, but never lightened. Caramel colouring must be added cautiously. A fair indication of the final colour can be found by removing a sample in a preheated pint beer glass. Add the concentrated colouring matter to the main wort until the correct shade is obtained.

Sweetex Liquid and other suitable artificial sweeteners are best added to the beer just prior to bottling. The actual amount must be apportioned according to taste.

"DARK ALE"

A sturdy Brown Ale, Full of body and flavour, balanced by the sweetness of lactose.

Ingredients for 4 gallons at a S.G. of 50

4½ lb. Crushed pale malt
6 oz. Flaked maize
6 oz. Crushed crystal malt
6 oz. Cracked black malt
12 oz. Lactose
1 lb. Soft dark brown sugar
1½ oz. Fuggles hops
Caramel colouring
Stout yeast.

Production information

Follow the basic method as given in chapter 3.

Water	Soft with added chlorides. Bias towards Potassium instead of Sodium Chloride if carbonate content is high
Mash pH	5·0–5·3
Water temperatures	Mix at 168°F to give an initial heat of 148–150°F
Mashing time	3 hours or overnight
Sparged wort	Collect 5 gallons at S.G. 30
Maximum possible extract	155 degrees
Hops	Select to 8 A.A.U.'s
Boiling	1½–2 hours
Final collected quantity	4¼ gallons at a S.G. of 50
Racking gravity	S.G. of 11–12.

BARLEY BROWN
Ingredients for 5 gallons of Brown Ale at a S.G. of 49

    6 lb. Crushed pale malt
    8 oz. Cracked roast malt
    8 oz. Cracked crystal malt
    2 lb. Demerara sugar
    1½ oz. Northern Brewer hops
    1 oz. Hallertau or Fuggles hops
    Top fermenting beer yeast
    Sweetex liquid to taste at bottling.

Production information—Follow the basic method.

Water and treatment as per the Dark Ale recipe

Mashing time	3 hours or overnight
Sparged wort	Collect 5¼ gallons at S.G. 33
Maximum possible extract	185 degrees
Boiling	1½–2 hours
Hops	Select to 13 A.A.U.'s
Final collected quantity	5¼ gallons at a S.G. of 49
Racking gravity	S.G. of 10–11.

McKINLAY
Ingredients for 4 gallons of sweet stout at a S.G. of 52

    5 lb. Crushed pale malt
    8 oz. Flaked maize
    8 oz. Cracked black malt
    2 lb. Malt extract (add as sugar to boiler)
    1 lb. Lactose
    1½ oz. Northern Brewer hops
    Top fermenting beer yeast.

Production information—Follow the basic method.

Water and treatment as per the Dark Ale recipe

Mashing time	3 hours or overnight
Sparged wort	Collect 4½ gallons at a S.G. of 35
Maximum possible extract	165 degrees
Hops	Select to 8 A.A.U.'s
Boiling	1½–2 hours
Final collected quantity	4¼ gallons at a S.G. of 49
Racking gravity	S.G. of 10–11.

BALTIC BLACK STOUT

"Baltic Black" is a medicinal stout with rather an acquired taste. The inclusion of Liquorice demands that it must be treated with respect!

Ingredients for 4 gallons at a S.G. of 46

6 lb. Crushed pale malt
8 oz. Flaked barley
6 oz. Cracked roast barley
3 oz. Cracked black malt
8 oz. Lactose
6 in. Stick of plain black Liquorice (chop small and add to boiler)
1 oz. Northern Brewer hops
Top fermenting beer yeast.

Production information

Follow the basic method

Water and treatmentas per the Dark Ale recipe

Mashing time	3 hours or overnight
Sparged wort	Collect 4½ gallons at S.G. of 43
Maximum possible extract	195 degrees
Hops	Select to 5 A.A.U.'s
Boiling	1½–2 hours
Final collected quantity	4¼ gallons at a S.G. of 46
Racking gravity	S.G. of 11–12.

CHAPTER 36

Irish stout

THERE is only one commercial Dry Stout worth noting: Guinness Extra Stout. This superb drink is recognised by millions throughout the world as one of the best beers ever brewed.

To brew a stout comparable with Guinness has been the elusive goal of home-brewers for years. Various recipes have been tried, but it still remains one of the few commercial beers that is rarely bettered by home-brewed beer. Good recipes have been formulated, but it is one beer that certainly cannot be brewed successfully from Malt Extract syrup. "Mashing" is essential.

The "real" drink demands highly technical brewing gear way out of reach of our dustbin breweries, especially regarding the head retention process. After many trials, I consider that my recipe for "Goodness Stout" is as near to draught Guinness as it is possible to brew on amateur equipment. Extra Pale Malt and a higher gravity have been formulated in the brew to compensate for our amateur limitations.

"GOODNESS STOUT"

Recipe for 5 gallons of "Goodness Stout"

    7 lb. Crushed pale malt
    1 lb. Cracked roast barley
    1 lb. Flaked barley
    1 oz. Bullion hops
    1½ oz. Keyworth Mid-Season or Northern Brewer

The characteristic malty flavour of Guinness is derived from the Roast Barley. I am surprised that this malt has not been brought into more general use in home brewing.

The flavour and colouring properties are far superior to black malt that is widely used in Stout recipes. Roast Barley is an absolute must for this recipe.

The Stout is such a heavy malty drink that traditional flavour hops would be wasted in this brew. Regarding dark beers, I am fully in favour of the modern trend of selecting hop rates on an Alpha Acid content rather than the old lb./barrel system. Alpha Acid is a measure of the hop bitterness. Using a blend of Bullion and Keyworth Mid-Season, it is possible to use only $\frac{1}{2}$ oz./gallon of hops for this very bitter beer. The latter hops may be difficult to obtain, but Northern Brewer act as a good substitute.

The brewing water is equally as important. Dublin and London waters are similar to many domestic supplies derived from chalk formations, and is classed as a moderately hard carbonate liquor. By boiling for a $\frac{1}{4}$ hour, most of this hardness can be precipitated out of solution to leave the water fairly soft. Moderately hard and hard waters need this treatment prior to mashing. Soft water could benefit from the addition of $\frac{1}{2}$ a level teaspoonful of chalk (calcium carbonate) to the 5 gallons to balance the acidity of the roast malt.

Method

Follow the basic method as given in chapter 3.

Water	Medium Soft with 60-80 p.p.m. of Chalk
Mash pH	5·0–5·2 adjust with chalk
Water temperature	Mix at 168°F to give an initial heat of 149–150°F
Mashing time	3 hours or overnight
Sparged wort	Collect 6 gallons at S.G. of 40
Maximum possible extract	240 degrees
Hops	Select to 18 A.A.U.'s
Boiling	Boil 1$\frac{1}{2}$–2 hours to reduce length to 5 gallons
Final collected gravity	Hop Sparge to collect 5$\frac{1}{4}$ gallons at an S.G. of 45
Racking gravity	S.G. of 11–12.

On draught

If you intend to barrel the entire brew for use on draught, it will be necessary to add some heading liquid to the cube. Initially, I was against adding artificial heading agents, but now, from experience, I have found that this is the only way to promote a fine creamy head. The recommended dose of Leigh Williams heading liquid is 1 teaspoonful per 4 gallons. I have cautiously increased this dose to 2½ teaspoonsful for the 5 gallon batch to achieve the correct texture in the creamy head.

After a week, rack into a 5 gallon pressure barrel and add 2 ounces of priming sugar before fitting the pressure injector unit. Leave the Stout to condition for at least a week before sampling.

Serve carefully. Draught stout is notoriously hard to pull and the slow drawing off creates an impatient thirst that enhances the sinking of the first pint. A drip tray is needed beneath the tap in order that the glass can be filled to within half an inch of the rim. It is easier to retrieve the Stout slops from a tray rather than from the lounge carpet! Try to fill the glass with the tap outlet below the surface of the Stout to assist in promoting a creamy head.

Stout can be bottled if desired so long as you observe the following modifications to the recipe. Do not use the quota of heading liquid unless you have a nice sideline in making foam fire extinguishers! One teaspoonful in the 5 gallons should not cause embarrassment.

At the polythene cube stage, check the gravity of the Stout regularly, and bottle when the gravity has remained constant for 1 week. The gravity may still be at S.G. 8 or 9 when this condition is satisfied. Bottle and prime with ½ a teaspoonful of sugar per pint. Mature at least a month before drinking.

CHAPTER 37

Barley wine

BARLEY WINE is the strongest beer made with an alcoholic strength approaching that of a table wine (8–10% v/v). The production techniques are novel in so much that they embrace methods devised and established centuries ago. What we call Barley Wine was the everyday beer of these times, and starting gravities of between 80 and 100 were commonplace. It was usual to brew 2 beers from each wort. The rich wort was run off after mashing without sparging, and collected, and put to one side. The spent grains were then sparged to wash out a lighter gravity wort. Hence 2 lengths were obtained. The initial wort was then boiled with the hops to produce the "Ale" and the weaker running subsequently used to brew "Small Beer"; an inferior beer with a starting gravity of about 30. Nearly all the commercial beers brewed nowadays would be classed as inferior "Small Beers" by this rating!

Our production methods must follow these traditional ways if we wish to brew a high gravity ale. The system demands an understanding of the effect of sparging on the mashed grains, and also some skill in controlling it to suit your particular requirements. Careful collection of the sparged wort can mean that we can also brew 2 beers from 1 mash, and this is why I have grouped "Barley Wine" with "Shandy". The advantage with this arrangement is that you can brew a length of beer specifically for your wife or kids. Kids love the thought of dad brewing some beer just for them, and really no harm is done since these second runnings rarely have starting gravity greater than an S.G. of 20.

Knowing when to stop the sparging for the Barley Wine wort to prevent dilution needs extra attention. The best method is to float a hydrometer and thermometer in the collected wort. The temperature will be between 140 and 150°F and using the correction table on Page 148, the true gravity of wort can be estimated. If, for instance, a wort of S.G. 50 is required then this will give a lower reading if the temperature is say 150°F then sparging must desist when the wort reading is 50 divided by the correction factor for 150°F, that is, stop sparging when the gravity reading is

$$\frac{50}{2 \cdot 15} = 23 \cdot 3$$

With 20° of added sugar and after boiling the gravity will be raised to about an S.G. of 80. Brewery yeasts are not usually very happy in the high alcohol environment produced by these ales and hence it is better to use a good wine yeast.

Conduct the primary fermentation as for lower gravity beers and rack off into gallon jars with airlocks. Do not add finings, but carefully rack the beer off the sediment after 2 weeks and then 3 more times at 4 monthly intervals. Take care to exclude as much air as possible during these rackings. If there is any doubt over the quality of the fermented wort do not risk it for the long maturation period. The higher starting gravity will mean that for normal mashing temperatures the beer will end up fairly sweet. Low temperature mashes are therefore recommended for certain recipes to overcome this characteristic.

CELEBRATION ALE

3 gallons at S.G. 75

> 7 lb. Crushed pale malt
> 1 lb. Flaked rice
> 4 oz. Cracked crystal malt
> 2 oz. Cracked wheat malt
> 1 lb. White sugar
> ½ lb. Demerara sugar
> 1 oz. Hallertau or W.G.V. or Progress hops
> 3 oz. Golding hops
> Formula 67 yeast.

Mash the mixed grist at 148°F in permanently hard water for 3 hours with the pH nearer 5·2 than 5·0. Sparge until the specific gravity (corrected for temperature) of the total collected wort falls to 50. Normal sparging conditions should satisfy this gravity check after 3½ gallons have been drawn off. Separate this rich wort and continue sparging to retrieve the rest of the sugar retained by the goods. Another 3½ gallons can be collected yielding a gravity of just over 20. The division must be determined by the specific gravity of the first fraction and not by the guideline quantities.

Add the sugar and hops to the barley wine wort and boil for just 1 hour.

Strain off and restore the volume to just over 3 gallons. Pitch with a Formula 67 yeast starter when cool to 70°F. Ferment 7–10 days, cleaning the yeast crop as necessary until the gravity falls to 15. Rack off into gallon jars and fit airlocks with rubber bungs. Do not add finings. After a further 2 weeks rack off from the sediment into other gallon jars taking great pains to exclude as much air as possible. Add 1 teaspoonful of stock sterilising solution (or 1 Campden Tablet) to each gallon to ward off oxidisation and infection.

Repeat the racking procedure twice more at 4 monthly intervals. The last time omit the sterilising solution and "Krausen" the beer using a ½ teaspoonful of Formula 67 yeast creamed into the bulk. Bottle in "nips" or ¼ pints priming each with the equivalent of ½ a teaspoonful of white sugar per pint.

Mature for 6 months before drinking.

SHANDY

Approximately 3½ gallons of wort
(Second running from Celebration Ale)

½ oz. Golding Hops
1 teaspoonful Vanilla Essence
Pared rind of 2 lemons (No pith or juice)
Caramel colouring to suit.

Boil the second running of the Celebration Ale within ½ hour. Increase the depth of colour with caramel solution if desired.

Strain off and ferment with Formula 67 yeast until the gravity drops to an S.G. or 2 or 3. Rack off into a closed container and fine with gelatine. Adjust the sweetness with Sweetex Liquid or Lactose to suit and bottle priming each as per normal beer.

The Shandy is ready for drinking after only a week

"KIEVE"

2 gallons at a Starting Gravity of 73

A Barley Wine Strength Irish Stout

7 lb. 3 oz. Crushed pale malt
2 lb. Flaked barley
12 oz. Roast barley
50% Bullion hops
15% Keyworth mid-season $\left.\right\}$ Select to give 3·5
35% Mixed hops $\qquad$ A.A.U.'s per gallon

Mash at 145°F for 3 hours in soft water slightly chalked to give a pH of around 5·2. Sparge to collect 150 degrees of extract (i.e. volume × S.G. = 150 after temperature correction).

The rest of the procedure is the same as for the Celebration Ale recipe. Second runnings can be used for Shandy production.

If mashed at 149°F this brew makes a very interesting Stout if all the wort is collected and the normal Stout procedure followed to give a 6 or 7 gallon batch with a starting gravity of 43·5°.

APPENDIX I

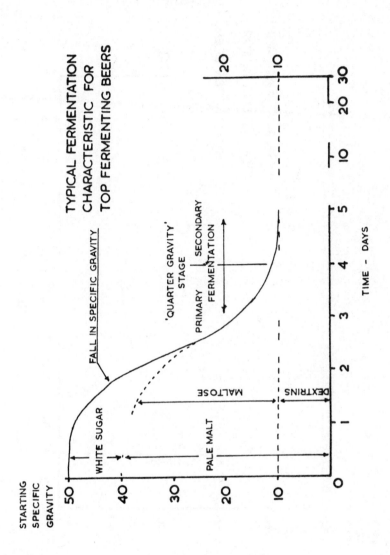

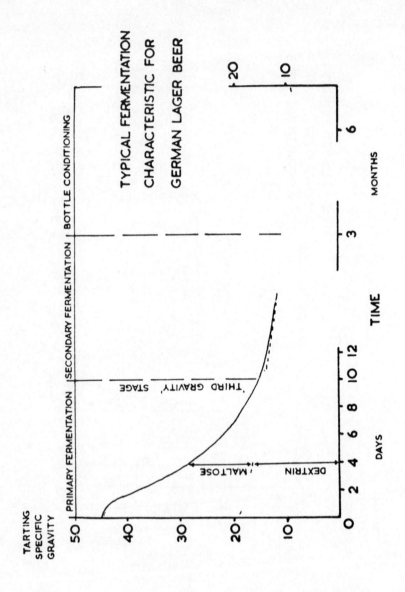

TYPICAL FERMENTATION CHARACTERISTIC FOR GERMAN LAGER BEER

CONVERSION TABLES

The recipes in this book have been given in the traditional English or Imperial system. Brewing beer at home is rapidly becoming a world-wide hobby and as such it is essential to to cater for the thirsts of our colleagues in far away lands.

I enjoy my 'pint' of best bitter and no doubt I will enjoy it just as much when I have got to ask for 0.586 litre of the same brew when we have finally 'gone metric' in a few years time!

Conversion tables have been included to satisfy English, Metric, and U.S.A. systems of measurement. Don't try to be too exacting over the calculations since for most practical purposes, it is quite acceptable to round off the figures. For instance, when converting 1 lb. to metric units, 450 gms. is near enough rather than the quoted equivalent of 453 gms.

WEIGHT   *British to Metric*

	5 lb.	= 2.267 kilogrammes
	4 lb.	= 1.814 kilos
	3 lb.	= 1.360 kilos
	2 lb.	= 907 grammes
	1 lb.	= 453 gms.
	½ lb.	= 226 gms.
	¼ lb.	= 113 gms.
	1 oz.	= 30 gms. (approx.)
Tablespoon	½ oz.	= 15 gms. (approx.)
Dessertspoon	¼ oz.	= 10 gms. (approx.)
Teaspoon	⅛ oz.	= 5 gms. (approx.)

Metric to British

5 kilogrammes	= 11 lb.
4 kilos	= 8 lb. 12 ozs.
3 kilos	= 6 lb. 9 ozs.
2 kilos	= 4 lb. 6 ozs.
1 kilo	= 2 lb. 3 ozs.
500 grammes	= 1 lb. 1½ ozs.
250 gms.	= 8¾ ozs.
125 gms.	= 4½ ozs.
100 gms.	= 3½ ozs.
50 gms.	= 1½ ozs.

CAPACITY

British to Metric

	1 gallon	=	4.546 litres
		=	4546 millilitres (or c.c.s.)
	1 pint	=	568 ml/ccs.
	½ pint	=	284 ml/ccs.
	1 fl. oz.	=	28 ml/ccs.
Tablespoon	½ fl. oz.	=	15 ml/ccs. (approx.)
Dessertspoon	¼ fl. oz.	=	10 ml/ccs. (approx.)
Teaspoon	⅛ fl. oz.	=	5 ml/ccs. (approx.)

Metric to British

5 litres	=	8 pints 14 ozs.
4½ litres	=	7 pints 18 ozs.
4 litres	=	7 pints
3 litres	=	5 pints 5 ozs.
2 litres	=	3 pints 10 ozs.
1 litre	=	1 pint 14 ozs.
500 millilitres	=	17 ozs.
250 ml/ccs.	=	8½ ozs.
125 ml/ccs.	=	4¼ ozs.
100 ml/ccs.	=	3½ ozs.
50 ml/ccs.	=	1¾ ozs.

253

Sugar, castor, 60
— cube, 60
— dark, 61
— demerara, 61
— granulated, 60
— icing, 60
— invert, 61
— white, 60
Sulphates, 99
Sulphur Dioxide, 113
Syrups, 63
Sweetex Liquid, 63, 234, 244
Sweet Stouts, 233
— Black Beauty, 42
— McKinlay, 236

Tannin, 212
Teaspoon, 95
Temperature control, 13, 33, 47, 139
Temporary Hardness, 91
Testing for pH, 39, 48
— starch, 46, 139
Thermometer, 32, 135
Tincture of Iodine, 140
Top fermentation, 130
Torrefied barley, 58
Treacle, 63
Treatment, acid, 86
— water, 102

Ullage, 194
Utilisation of Hops, 81

Verticillium Wilt, 74, 76

Water, 83
— Analysis, 90
— Authorities, 85
— Domestic, 85
— For Lager, 225
— Hardness of, 90
— Sources of brewing, 85
— Treatment, 84, 86, 102
Wheat, Malt, 59
— Syrup, 59
Whitbread 'B' Strain yeast 108
Whitbread Golding Variety Hops, 76
White Sugar, 60, 175
Wild Hops, 67
— yeasts, 212
Wilt, Verticillium, 74, 76
Wine Filtering powder, 166
Wort, 18, 21, 65

Yeast, 21, 106, 163
— Bakers, 106
— Bite, 162
— Bottom fermenting, 197, 225
— Brewers, 106
— Classification, 226
— Commercial, 108
— Cultures, 108, 109
— Formula 67, 243
— Lager, 167, 176, 225
— Saving, 109
— Starter, 107, 207
— Top fermenting, 176, 197, 225
— Wild, 212
— Wine, 242

Other "AW" Books

FIRST STEPS IN WINEMAKING
The acknowledged introduction to the subject. Unbeatable at the price.
C. J. J. Berry
SCIENTIFIC WINEMAKING—made easy
The most advanced and practical textbook on the subject.
J. R. Mitchell, L.I.R.C., A.I.F.S.T.
THE WINEMAKER'S COOKBOOK
Gives a whole range of exciting dishes using your home-made wine.
Tilly Timbrell and Bryan Acton
WINEMAKING AND BREWING
The theory and practice of winemaking and brewing in detail.
Dr. F. W. Beech and Dr. A. Pollard
GROWING GRAPES IN BRITAIN
Indispensable handbook for winemakers whether they have six vines or six thousand.
Gillian Pearkes
"AMATEUR WINEMAKER" RECIPES
Fascinatingly varied collection of over 200 recipes.
C. J. J. Berry
WINEMAKING WITH CANNED AND DRIED FRUIT
How to make delightful wines from off the supermarket shelf.
C. J. J. Berry
PRESERVING WINEMAKING INGREDIENTS
Includes drying, chunk bottling, deep freezing, chemical preservation, etc.
T. Edwin Belt
HOME BREWING SIMPLIFIED
Detailed recipes for bottled and draught beer plus know how.
RECIPES FOR PRIZEWINNING WINES
Produce superb wines for your own satisfaction!
Bryan Acton
WHYS AND WHEREFORES OF WINEMAKING
Assists the winemaker to *understand* what he is doing.
THE WINEMAKER'S GARDEN
All you need to know about planting the garden for winemaking.
Duncan Gillespie
HOW TO MAKE WINES WITH A SPARKLE
Discover the secrets of producing Champagne-like wine of superb quality.
J. Restall and D. Hebbs
130 NEW WINEMAKING RECIPES
Superb collection of up-to-date recipes
C. J. J. Berry

Send for current price list

MAKING WINES LIKE THOSE YOU BUY
Imitate commercial wines at a fraction of what they would cost to buy.
Bryan Acton and Peter Duncan

THE GOOD WINES OF EUROPE
A simple guide to the names, types and qualities of wine.
Cedric Austin

ADVANCED HOME BREWING
The most advanced book on home brewing available in this country.
Ken Shales

PROGRESSIVE WINEMAKING
500 pages, from scientific theory to the production of quality wines at home.
Peter Duncan and Bryan Acton Paperback, Hard cover

HOME BREWED BEERS AND STOUTS
The first and still recognised as the best book on this fascinating subject.
C. J. J. Berry

WOODWORK FOR WINEMAKERS
Make your own wine press, fermentation cupboard, fruit pulper, bottle racks, etc.
C. J. Dart and D. A. Smith

BREWING BETTER BEERS
Explains many finer points of brewing technique.
Ken Shales

HINTS ON HOME BREWING
Concise and basic down to earth instructions on home brewing.
C. J. J. Berry

MAKING MEAD
The only full-length paperback available on this winemaking speciality.
Bryan Acton and Peter Duncan

PLANTS UNSAFE FOR WINEMAKING
—includes native and naturalised plants, shrubs and trees.
T. Edwin Belt

BREWING BEERS LIKE THOSE YOU BUY
Over 100 recipes from around the world. Brew your own favourite brand.
D. Line

COMMONSENSE WINEMAKING
Practical no frills primer in winemaking
Anne Parrack

THE HAPPY BREWER
Caters for the home brewer who wishes to go more deeply into the theory of brewing.
Wilf Newsom

Send for current price list